Dear

For Lisa foxc
fabulous 50

GW00362242

The Magnificent Seven
Plus ONE

A BEAUTIFUL MEDIA PUBLICATION
ATLANTA, GEORGIA
404.847.0282

by the
"Beautiful People"

BEAUTIFUL MEDIA

5652 Kingsport Drive

Atlanta, GA 30342

404-847-0282

Fax 404-847-9748

Library of Congress Cataloging Number: 2004108135

ISBN: 0-9755398-0-9

Printed in the United States of America

First soft cover printing by Beautiful Media May 2004

Graphic Design by Bonnie G. Menoni

Most Beautiful Media books are available at special quantity discounts for bulk purchase for sales promotions, premiums, fund raising, and educational needs. Special books or book excerpts can also be created to fit specific needs. For details, call (404) 847-0282 or write Beautiful Media, 5652 Kingsport Drive, Atlanta, Georgia U.S.A. 30342.

To Lisa
we are so proud
To call you our
friend, Have a fab 50th
much love
Steve + tracy
xx   xx

Dear Lisa
We love you &
really appreciate
your friendship
& the kind-times
here's to many
more
love & John
Ali x.

To my gorgeous Lisa
I'M so happy
to have you
as my wife
Hope you've
enjoyed
your day
love you lots
Mark
x x

To Lisa,
A lady full of life,
love, & laughter it
so glad we enjoy it
with you, much love Tom
Rob & Kerry
x x x

In Memory of

Rachel, Beth

and

Peggy

ACKNOWLEDGMENTS

To my publisher extraordinaire, Katherine P. To amazing Nancy M. and all the KD's. To my dearest Kentucky friends, particularly Jeanette S., Mary D., Jane S., Pat D., Donnie C., Wade and Nancy P. and Brooks and Marilyn B. To my many Ohio friends especially, my Columbus angels Lisa P., Jeanne S., Laura K., Kathy K., Mike R., Beth S., Susie S., Besty A., and the special, amazingly supportive Brookside girls and guys. To the unique and skillful CWDGA women. To my dear friends in pageantry. To the beautiful people of Marco Island, Florida especially Jolé F., Sharon H., yoga ladies, Faye M., Homer and Phyllis R. and to Kimberly D. in New York. To my special friends in volunteerism who share my passion, especially CHL, HFF, LC, LW and THE BABE. To all those talented reporters, editors and producers who have taught me so much.

To those in heaven who live in my heart forever…Peggy, Rachel, Beth, Karen, Tommy and Bud.

To my adopted family, the Glanzman's, especially my wonderful stepchildren, Vanessa, Mike and his wife Heidi as well as their daughters, Gretchen and Samantha. To my family Darby, Bill,

Logan, Lana, and my Texas cousins. To my precious parents, Julie and Hal. To my uniquely spectacular daughters, Hallie, Stacey and Billi. To the happiest, most self-confident man I have ever known, my beloved husband, Gary. You have each given me the love and confidence to pursue a life I could never have imagined.

And to my God who has forever been my light!

Thank you and Love to You-all,

Donna Hazle Glanzman

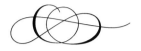

"If a man happens

to find himself,

he has a mansion

he can inhabit

with dignity all

the days of his life."

James Michener

Table of Contents

PREFACE

In the early sixties, a movie called *The Magnificent Seven* was a highly successful western. It was the story of seven American gunslingers who became mercenary defenders of a small Mexican village being terrorized by bandits. The American protectors found themselves doing more than just keeping the locals from being robbed. They showed the Mexicans how to defend themselves and be strong. They willingly inspired the villagers to focus on their importance to their families and friends as they learned to protect themselves.

As I began my speaking career, I realized that people can be motivated when they discover themselves and appreciate their uniqueness. I wanted to share the art of finding the inner qualities that would ensure that each person can be his or her own inspiration. The Americans in *The Magnificent Seven* were able to bring out the power of the individual. This book...first conceived as a speech...reveals the art of discovering inspiration from within. My Magnificent Seven imperatives, PLUS ONE most powerful truism, will transform your life.

My life has been filled with so many stories. It is a tapestry woven with memories of extraordinary events and amazingly special people. I have faced life with childlike faith and, even now, in my fifties, I continue to walk wide-eyed through my days knowing that there are still innumerable adventures awaiting me.

Each of us has a philosophy we live by. We have a need to believe in something. We seek a foundation upon which we make our decisions. We fall back on these beliefs as rationale for what we are about to do and what we choose not to do. I believe without any doubt that God has led me at each turn, just like a guide in a deep cavern who shines a light in the darkness. Sometimes when I have been shattered by my own missteps or circumstances in my world, He has even carried me through the pain.

Yes, we are beings of free-will. We were created that way so we must find out how to live with value, substance and faith.

I do not write this book because I have all the answers. I write it because I am committed to certain "imperatives" that have made my life fulfilled. They are the core of my conscience, my decisions, and my actions. They are the basis for my beliefs. There are, I believe, seven of these plus ONE that pull all of life together into a meaningful form. They truly are magnificent in their ability to define our lives and to focus our motives. They are tied together by a faith in God!

At the twilight of our being, we will look back at what use we made of our talents, our loves and our dreams. What a travesty it would be to feel disappointed at what we see! I am determined that I will be smiling...that my life has made a difference to those I touched and that when gone, there will be a small hole in the universe where I once stood.

It is my guess that you have chosen this book because you, too, are searching for your own place and significance in this world. You won't be disappointed with what you find as long as you stay true to yourself, accepting of these *MAGNIFICENT SEVEN* and faithful to the God who made it all!

As you read on, remember that life is filled with doors that open and close...sometimes right in our faces...and that what really matters in life can seldom be etched on a trophy. Remember also, that things are not always what they seem. That you are your greatest caregiver. That believing in yourself requires knowing yourself. That no matter what your age, dreams are a necessity of life. That surrounding yourself with people who understand, care and support you is key. That without the valleys of life, you will never appreciate the mountaintops. And, the most important thing, there is a God in this world, and it is not you or me!

There you have it...life in a nutshell! But, how do I know these things and why would anyone want to read what I think? Two very excellent questions, and you will have your own answer soon. But, for now, let me say that I am a survivor, fiercely protective of those I love, strong willed, persistent, competitive, sensitive, ornery sometimes, anxious to be accepted and loved, weird, highly opinionated and truly committed to those in need. But, most importantly, I am a storyteller who is compelled to share what I have learned.

I am also a tour-guide. We will be journeying through your life, and I will point out treasures that you may possess already or long to have. At the end, you will find your own story and be amazed at all you have seen. I write this book because I believe I can help you understand your place in this world more completely.

We each have a mission in life. In fact, I believe we spend our whole lifetime searching for why we are here and for what we are meant to do. I have found that meaning, I think, and it is to teach the lessons of life that I have learned. It is my wish that what I share with you here will help you discover the inspiration within yourself. And once discovered, you will be rewarded with an understanding of why you are on this earth!!

So, my friend, since you are focused on my words, right here, right now, then I would say we are ready to begin our journey.

May God bless you as you take this first step.

CHAPTER ONE

Value What Really Matters!

*"What you love is a sign from your higher
self of what you are to do."*

Sanaya Roman
Author

*"Man looks at the outward appearance,
but the Lord looks at the heart."*

The Book of Samuel

> *"The use of money is*
> *all the advantage there*
> *is in having money."*
>
> Benjamin Franklin
> Inventor, Politician

The affluent young couple looked around their home for the last time. It had only been three years since they had moved their four young children into their two million-dollar mansion. It was a marriage filled with country clubs, private schools, luxurious cars and extravagant jewelry. There was also the second home...a million dollar condo on Singer Island in Florida...and the most expensive furnishings available. Always wearing the best and latest fashions, this couple had it all! Then, the wife heard of another city near the mountains that she loved. She wanted to move there, to a home even bigger, near more influential people, throwing swankier parties.

It didn't matter that her children and her husband were being torn from their friends...that her husband's businesses were in the area they were leaving. All that mattered was that she just knew she would finally be happy in this new place .

So, there they stood, looking for the last time at the home they had planned and designed and spent two years building. They shut the door behind them and headed off to their new city.

Three months later, with movie stars, millionaires and rich successful entrepreneurs for neighbors and parents of their children's classmates, this couple was not speaking. They felt lost in all the grandeur.

What had they expected when they acquired so many "things?" Where was their focus? What did they value? An overloaded life, filled with fabulous things, can be amazingly seductive.

This couple began looking around for reasons why their money did not seem to bring them happiness. They became the epitome of Henry David Thoreau's thoughts, "If you have built castles in the air, your work need not be lost; that is where it should be. Now put the foundations under them!"

They listened as the minister at a neighbor's church proclaimed that according to the Bible, the only way to break the power of money was to be comfortable giving it away. They saw homeless; they saw sick children. They decided that together they would make a difference. The successful young couple began donating 10% of their fortune to charity every year. Their success still touches so many. Today, they realize that in giving they have received the greatest gift...valuing what really matters.

MONEY...THAT MUST BE A KEY
FAME...THAT MUST BE THE KEY
WINNING...THAT MUST BE THE KEY
WHAT DOES REALLY MATTER?

Cartoons and comic strips have so often been the outlet and the acceptable avenue for social comment. Take that cute little guy in Peanuts. What a philosopher and genius Charles Schultz was! He didn't really care to address the pressing issues of arms control or stock market scandals. His pursuit was the search for what really matters in life.

"You have to count on living every single day in a way you believe will make you feel good about your life."
Jane Seymour
Actress

So, Charles Schultz presented some questions for his audience's consideration. What follows is a loosely paraphrased version of his quiz. Let's see how you do. Take your time and be sure to keep your score. You WILL be graded later.

1. Name the last five winners of the Nobel Peace prize.

2. Give the name of the winners in the 2001 and 2002 Best Actor and Best Actress categories of the Academy Awards.

3. List the top five men and women golfers of 1997.

4. Name the 1958, 1968, 1978, 1988 and 1998 Miss Americas.

5. Give the names of five winners of the Heisman trophy in the last ten years and where they play football now.

6. The five best selling authors in 2003 were...

How did you do? Did you have the urge to reach for some written help or call a good friend who remembers everything including what you were wearing ten years ago when you had lunch together?

My guess is that you failed miserably. Oh, maybe you got one or two. I mean, we would all get Tiger Woods and Tom Clancy, but really, how did you do? The answers include people who have worked their entire lives to reach the pinnacle of success in their chosen fields, yet we cannot even remember their names. What does that mean?

Now ask yourself these questions....

1. Name the five people who have made the biggest difference in your life.

2. List three teachers that changed the direction you were heading.

3. Give four names of people that you would always help when they need it.

4. Name two people who have impacted the course of your career or your personal life.

5. List three people whom you call real friends.

6. Write down the most important one person in your life.

How did you do on this quiz? My guess is you were 100% correct. Why? These people made a difference in YOUR life. They may have never had one moment's recognition in the world of media or the world of competitions, but they are TRUE winners just the same.

> *"The mind grows by what it feeds on."*
> Josiah G. Holland
> Author, Educator

The affect our teachers (usually on the list of those who made a difference) have on each of us can never be underestimated. Think of those names you just listed for question number two above. Why did you think of them? As a junior high, high school and college instructor, I know the uniqueness of the teaching experience.

- **Real teachers can't walk past a crowd of kids without straightening up the line.**
- **Real teachers can predict exactly what parents show up at Open House.**
- **Real teachers have their best conferences in the parking lot.**
- **Real teachers know it is better to seek forgiveness than to ask for permission.**
- **Real teachers know that rules do not apply to them.**
- **Real teachers have never heard an original excuse.**
- **Real teachers understand the importance of making sure every kid gets a Valentine.**
- **Real teachers hear the heartbeats of crisis.**
- **Real teachers always have time to listen.**
- **Real teachers know they teach students, not subjects.**
- **Real teachers are absolutely nonexpendable**
AND
- **Real teachers never stop teaching no matter what they are doing!**

We mold ourselves dependent upon the focus we have. Some of us choose where to look. Others are like the children playing "Blind Man's Bluff"…we are blindfolded and spun around in a circle by life's events. The blindfold is suddenly yanked off of our eyes, and we are supposed to know which way to look for what is meaningful.

According to Rick Warren, author of **The Purpose Driven Life**, "Without a clear purpose, you have no foundation on which to base decisions, allocate your time or use your resources."

Ask yourself the following questions...

What will your best friend, your spouse, and your children say is important to you?

What do you SAY is important to you?

Whose opinions do you value and seek?

Where do you get your information and your news?

Who do you choose to believe?

Where do you spend your time?

Recently, I had a disagreement with a friend of thirty years. As we spent hours and, I must admit, weeks trying to sort out the problem, I was astounded by her opinion of me. What she thought was of value to me was nowhere close to what I believed in. I was shocked. She had known me all these years...had been my "best friend," yet the person she saw was not even remotely the person I thought I was, and, interestingly not the person that people I had befriended in the past four or five years saw. What did that mean? I began some serious introspection. I found that self-examination needs to be an habitual exercise; otherwise valuing what really matters may be overshadowed by the world's temptations.

Try asking a longtime, close friend to be brutally honest with you about what they see when they see you. Don't be afraid. It will be a chance to gain some encouragement, or like me, you will be astounded by the interpretation of your actions. I realized that some of the messages I had been sending did not reflect my true self. I didn't like what my best friend was seeing. I knew it was time to focus inward. My heart and mind were not being well represented to my friend. Maybe I was like Job in the Old Testament, "I have labored to no purpose; I have spent my strength in vain and for nothing."

Have you had moments of self-reflection lately? Have you studied where you seem to be moving in your life? There is no better moment than right now to do that. Let's start with money and time. For as you know "where your focus...there too your heart."

Imagine someone is going to give you $86,400 each day. This money all has to be spent in one day. You can't save the money or hold it over to the next day for a big purchase. You can't borrow from tomorrow for today. You can only have your $86,400 today. If you don't use it all, too bad! It gets thrown away...it's totally wasted.

But tomorrow, you will get $86,400 again. What a deal!

What would you do? DRAW out every cent, of course! Everyone has such a bank. And, the name of this bank is TIME!

Every morning it credits you with 86,400 seconds. Every night it writes off as lost whatever of this you failed to invest to good purpose. It carries over no balance. It allows no overdraft. Each day it opens a new account for you. Each night it burns the remains of the day. If you fail to use the day's deposits, the loss is yours. There is no going back. There is no drawing against "tomorrow." You must live in the present on today's deposits. Invest it so as to get from it the most in health, happiness and success. The clock is ticking. Make the most of today. To realize the value of...

ONE YEAR, ask a student who has failed a grade

ONE MONTH, ask a mother who has given birth to a premature baby

ONE WEEK, ask an editor of a weekly newspaper

ONE DAY, ask a daily wage laborer who has kids to feed

ONE MINUTE, ask a person who has missed a train

ONE SECOND, ask a person who has avoided an accident

ONE MILLI-SECOND, ask a person who has won a
SILVER medal, not GOLD, in the Olympics

YESTERDAY IS HISTORY...TOMORROW IS A MYSTERY...TODAY IS A GIFT. THAT IS WHY IT IS CALLED THE PRESENT!

Now, look at your life. Where do your minutes go?

When do you wish you had more time in the day...and WHY?

This is your 86,400 second gift. Looking realistically at where you spend your time is the key to what matters to you. The more time you spend, the more important the issue.

Are you satisfied with your life? Do you find yourself envying what someone else has? Do you think your spouse or significant other or child needs to lose weight or change their hair color or make more money?

"Before you can value what really matters, you must know where you spend your time. Once you have looked AND written it down, decide whether you like it or not! Then, change what you don't."

Donna Glanzman
Author

Why is it so many of us never seem to be satisfied? I believe it is healthy and valuable to seek improvement in our lives and in the lives of those we love. But, it is the motive that determines the outcome. Ecclesiastes says that the basic motives for success are the driving forces of envy and jealousy. Do we try to change others because it makes our lives easier to manage? Or do we try to change them because we value their greatest assets and want to see them reach their goals? Or do we push and nag because we want to keep up with the Joneses or the Smiths or whomever?

Look closely at yourself…are you dissatisfied? Can you assess why?

Are you led by God or are you driven by motives you may not even understand?

Can you appreciate where you are at this moment in life? Expand on your thought.

Are you ready to handle the changes and challenges that are an everyday part of life's progression?

Consider this…

If the earth's population were shrunken into a village of just 100 people with all the human ratios existing in the world, what would that diverse village look like?

IN A ONE HUNDRED PERSON VILLAGE…

57 would be Asian
21 would be European
14 would be from the Western Hemisphere
8 would be African

IN A HUNDRED PERSON VILLAGE…

52 would be female
48 would be male
70 would be non-white
30 would be Christian
89 would be heterosexual
11 would be homosexual

IN A HUNDRED PERSON VILLAGE...

89 would live in substandard housing

70 would be unable to read

50 would suffer from malnutrition

1 would be near death

1 would have a college degree

1 would own a computer

IN A HUNDRED PERSON VILLAGE...

6 would possess 59% of the entire world's wealth, AND all six would be from the United States.

THINK ABOUT THIS...

If you live in a good home, have plenty to eat and can read, you are a member of a very select group.

If you live in a good home, have food, can read and own a computer, you are among the very elite.

If you have food in the refrigerator, clothes on your back, a roof over your head and a place to sleep...you are richer than 75% of the people in this world.

If you have money in the bank, in your wallet and spare change in a dish someplace, you are among the top 8% of the world's wealthy.

If you woke up this morning with more health than illness, you are more fortunate than the million people who will not survive this week.

If you have never experienced the danger of battle, the loneliness of imprisonment, the agony of torture or the pangs of starvation, you are ahead of 500 million people in the world.

If you can read this message, you are blessed more than two billion people in the world who cannot read at all.

If you can hold your head up with a smile on your face and are truly thankful...you are blessed because you can offer a healing touch.

Where do you fit in this Village of 100? Do you feel privileged? Are you valuing your position in this world more now? Do you see yourself focused on those who are wealthier than you or those who would look to you as their ideal? What do you believe really matters?

Remember our stunningly rich young couple? Before September 11, 2001, there were so many people believing like they did at first.

Money, possessions, power and prestige were what really mattered in life. Many of us walked through our days focused on our jobs or our homes, our golf games or our cars. We either looked at our loved ones, but saw right through them, or we rushed through dinners and fought over our desserts about meaningless issues. Then, two planes plowed into the very symbols of our power and wealth. Unbelievably, we saw the faces of the strangers frantically searching for those who were lost. People who had never thought their goals were wrong were questioning their focus. These people…all of us…were shaken to the core by the horrible reality that so much of what we strive for and save for and spend will not help us as we face crisis. Those who had not been sure where God fit into their lives or IF He even fit in "at all" openly begged for miracles.

On September 24, 2002, Mr. Cornel Nistorescu published the following article about America in the Romanian newspaper, *Evenimentulzilei*.

AN ODE TO AMERICA

Why are Americans so united? They would not resemble one another even if you painted them all in one color!

They speak all the languages of the world and form an astonishing mixture of civilizations and religious beliefs. Still, the American tragedy turned three hundred million people into a hand put on the heart.

Nobody rushed to accuse the White House, the army, and the secret service that they are a bunch of losers. Nobody rushed to empty their bank accounts. Nobody rushed out into the streets nearby to gape about. The Americans volunteered to donate blood and to give a helping hand.

After the first moments of panic, they raised their flag over the smoking ruins, putting on T-shirts, caps and ties in the colors of the national flag.

They placed their flags on buildings and cars as if in every place and on every car a government official or the president was passing.

On every occasion, they started singing their traditional song: "God Bless America!"

I watched the live broadcast and rerun after rerun for hours listening to the story of the guy who went down one hundred floors with a woman in a wheelchair without knowing who she was or of the California hockey player who gave his life fighting with the terrorists and prevented the plane from hitting a target that could have killed other hundreds or thousands of people.

How on earth were they able to respond united as one human being?

Imperceptibly, with every word and musical note, the memory of some turned into a modern myth of tragic heroes. And, with every phone call, millions and millions of dollars were put in a collection aimed at rewarding not man or family, but a spirit, which no money can buy.

What on earth can unite the Americans in such a way? Their Land? Their galloping History? Their economic Power? Money? I tried for hours to find an answer, humming songs and murmuring phrases at the risk of sounding commonplace. I thought things over, but I reached only one conclusion…Only FREEDOM can work such miracles!

We in America need to remember what really matters in life. Time has passed since that tragic September 11 day and many of us have become a bit immuned to, maybe even forgetful of, the horror that occurred that day. It brought us to our collective knees, but it became the rekindling of the spirit that has made our country what it is. For the first time in a long while, we valued what really mattered. We need to always hold on to that feeling and put it at the forefront of our lives.

THE ARTIFICIAL HEART

In 1984, Dr. William DeVries arrived at Humana Hospital Audubon in Louisville, Kentucky. He came with as much fanfare and publicity as a conquering hero, for, in fact, that is exactly what he was. He had been the first man to implant the Jarvik-7 Permanent Artificial Heart into a human. "It would be the medical story of the century," some said. The planning that went into the media coverage for this procedure was nearly as intense as the training for the nurses, doctors and staff. As the PR and Marketing Director for the hospital, only two months into my job, this would be the experience of a lifetime. Little did I know how amazing and challenging it would be…not because of the sheer numbers of reporters, networks and stories that would be generated, but because of the scrambling for control, leadership and fame.

The glare of spotlights is an unmatched aphrodisiac. The need to be the center of attention brought unique and unexpected situations to what was already a challenging experience. Dr. Alan Lansing was the head of the Humana Heart Institute which had been established a year earlier. He was an amazingly skilled cardiovascular surgeon who was studying with Dr. William DeVries to qualify as an artificial implant surgeon. This was a highly experimental procedure and the Food and Drug Administration (FDA) was watching every move carefully. Dr. Lansing convinced the founders of Humana, David Jones and Wendell Cherry, that recruiting Dr. DeVries to join the Heart Institute Medical Staff would prove the commitment of the company to the future of heart care.

The motives of everyone were, I believe, truly humanitarian and genuine. There were patient advocates and skilled counselors for not only those receiving the implants, but also their families and staff. In the beginning, there were positive stories with emphasis on the heroic sacrifices being made by all involved especially the patients and the doctors. Barney Clark, the first recipient of the Permanent Artificial Heart, had given a legacy of unselfish sacrifice by accept-ing Dr. DeVries' offer to give him the new heart at the University of Utah in Salt Lake City. When DeVries arrived in Louisville, he brought the knowledge gained from his time caring for Dr. Clark.

On Thanksgiving weekend in 1984, after rigorous screenings and tests, the Louisville phase of the Permanent Artificial Heart Project began. William Schroeder had been selected to receive the heart at Humana Hospital Audubon.

There was so much media interest in the project that the Louisville Convention Center was rented to accommodate press needs. The Humana corporate PR team was charged with develop-ing and implementing a massive media plan. I was the point-person at the hospital and would become spokesperson as the years pro-gressed. Entire studios were set up to accommodate live shows, and a battery of phones was made available in the media room. At the hospital, a press center had been designed with every imaginable amenity and production device the reporters might need.

If this much was done for the media, you can just imagine how much thought, time and money were put into the actual medical procedure. Operating rooms and hundreds of hours of special training ensured the staff would be ready. A wide range of physician specialists were recruited to participate in the experiment as support for any issue or complication. The team commitment for the life of the patient and the success of the experiment was truly mind-boggling. The dollars invested far exceeded the early estimates of $1,000,000 per implant.

But, eventually, the differences in philosophies and levels of experience, combined with the lure of control among the project participants began to interfere with the real meaning of the program. There was no doubt that Bill Schroeder and each of the other three implant patients that followed him were receiving the absolute best care. However, critics began to imply that some of those involved were forgetting to focus on the second most important aspect of the Artificial Heart experiment…the valuable research results that would save lives in the future.

I am not quite sure when the tone of the project started to change. But, the once close bond between Dr. DeVries and Dr. Lansing began deteriorating as they jockeyed for position with the media…glowing when they were the center of attention, dismissive when they were not. Dr. Lansing, who had initially been the spokesperson in front of throngs of national and international media, was no longer the spokesperson these reporters wanted. They wanted the guy who actually held the scalpel. They wanted Dr. DeVries.

Eventually, the two doctors split, but like a quiet divorce, stayed under the same roof to continue the implants. The FDA was unhappy that Dr. DeVries had time for interviews and "20/20" specials with Barbara Walters, but not enough time to complete the technical study results for the prestigious medical journals like "JAMA" and "The New England Journal of Medicine."

Through all of this, I could see the inflation of egos and the mesmerizing lure of being the center of attention. I, too, lost myself in the project. I wanted to be the decision-maker, the point person, the guide for all who had to face the onslaught of reporters. When the corporate staff would step-in leaving me out, I let my ego supercede the better good of the project, and I often chose the spotlight over the hugs of my daughters living in a single-parent home.

Dr. DeVries and Dr. Lansing may have lost sight of their original goals. They were driven to be successful...to complete the seven implants promised by the FDA and have their patients survive outside the sterile environment of a hospital with their Artificial Hearts. They were discouraged by the ultimate results of the program as were others on the team. I believe Dr. DeVries and Dr. Lansing were evaluating what really matters in life and realizing that fame is fleeting. What lasts are our core values and our innate desire to find purpose...to make a difference in this world.

Within four years, the Artificial Heart experiment was stopped. Why? I contend the implants ended because there was no convincing research data that the project should continue and because the two partners were literally not speaking to each other.

I often wonder if the project would have been abandoned had everyone stayed focused on why it began in the first place. If humility and commitment to all involved had been of paramount importance, would the history of the Artificial Heart be any different?

It took a great deal of introspection to realize that the true power is not always being in the spotlight. In fact, the most powerful person is often the one who understands the players and ensures that their goals are met while quietly standing in the shadows.

Paradox..."He who is first shall be last," a solitary carpenter said as He stood atop a mount over two thousand years ago. No matter what the lessons learned, the message is clear. When you value what really matters in any situation, the results will be positive for all involved.

THE VALUE OF THREE

A mother looked at some old family pictures not knowing where to begin. How could she tell her daughters what their childhood had been like? They could remember so little, but wanted to know so much. This would be the best Christmas gift she had ever given them. This would be the story of each of their lives.

She rummaged through boxes of pictures. There was Hallie, her ruffled bonnet tied snuggly around her bald little head. She lay tummy down on the lap of her father, big green eyes sparkling into the camera and her puffy cheeks accentuating a hint of a smile. "I remember that day," the mother said outloud. "My sister Peggy was graduating from Hanover College."

A flood of memories overwhelmed her...the day her sister took her daughters horseback riding on their parents' farm. The weekend they spent boating on Lake Cumberland. The day her sister won fifth in the triathlon while mother and daughters proudly cheered her on. The time she sang "kumbaya" around the campfire. The trip they took to the World's Fair in Knoxville...the day the call came that Peggy had died.

How had her daughters survived the loss of their beloved aunt? Was it the same strength that had allowed them to survive the divorce and the persistent absence of their father?

Was there some resilience held deep within these wonderful girls that would ensure they could overcome whatever life would throw at them? Had the childhood she had given them been right after all?

The box of pictures had evolved into a room full of memories. Donna stared at the faces of the daughters she loved so remarkably. There was Stacey, her blue jeans falling off her little crossed legs and her tiny hand stubbornly poised just beneath her chin as she stared sternly into the camera. The beauty in her profile was already visible at only three. My giggling Billi...how she glowed in every picture. Her smile contagiously prompted her sisters to giggle back at "their Baby."

There they were, all strewn across the floor. The ballerinas and witches, the bunnies and gypsies, the beauty queen and the diver, the lacrosse player and the prom queen, the birthday parties and Christmas celebrations, the Easter egg hunts and the Thanksgiving dinners. Their lives were spread before her like a never-ending palette of remembrances, and she cried. Cried for the laughter and the joy they had shared. She cried because the memories were so vague, so fleeting, so clouded by phone calls and business meetings and events she had hoped would bring her happiness. Here before her lay the meaning of her life. Why had she looked for it in the eyes of strangers, of men she had dated and business associates she had sparred with? Why had she prayed for God to show her what He wanted her to achieve in life when here was her greatest achievement, her greatest gift?

How had her daughters survived their childhood? They had survived because they knew she loved them! They knew in their hearts even when she yelled or cried or fussed that she did it out of love. She did it believing that rules kept children safe and that mothers must fight to protect their young. She knew that any sacrifice was worthwhile if the outcome was the happiness and peace, success and safety of her children. But, most of all, she knew that God would protect these little girls as long as she believed He was walking beside her.

Now, as she looked at her fifty years and wondered what God had expected her to accomplish, she knew the answer. She was to love these daughters and give them life with all of its joys and its sorrows. Her reason for being had finally been found!!!!

How do I know this story so well? Because these are my daughters, and this is my story.

Look at your family...

How often do you share your feelings with those you love?

Have you ever made a gift rather than purchased one?

Do you give what you want or what they ask for?

Do you only see the mistakes not the successes?

You may not grasp what is of value in the midst of stress or over-commitment, but it is there, right in front of you. Look around. Take care not to miss what really matters. Remember this...when you are gone and those around you speak of your life, they will not talk about deals you have closed or clients you have won or even how much money you acquired. They will speak of your impact on those you knew and loved. What will they say mattered to you?

RITUAL

Dr. William Baker, my brother, contributed the following story...

The idea came late one evening during Rachel's bedtime ritual. He sat on the edge of her bed. Buried deep under the covers on an unusually cold autumn night, she hid the fact that she still enjoyed having her Dad "tuck her in."

The back scratches he gave were really quite nice, a pleasant combination of tickles and scratches just like his Mom had given him. But she was 14 now and in high school, and well, it's not a cool thing. And his singing, UGH! He was horrible.

He was always putting on some of that old stuff from when he was young. Tonight, and for the past several nights, they had been exploring James Taylor, and Rachel had to admit, she really liked "Fire and Rain." She sometimes listened to it after school when no one was around. The gentle guitar and the haunting story were strangely attractive to her as it had been for Bill's entire generation in the early 70's.

But, he would sing along, and he would try to hit the notes, and he would get so close. So close that he was really bad! So bad, she scrunched under the covers to fight back the laughter, eyelids heavy, the song coming

Value What Really Matters!

to an end. *Now, it was her turn. He would start off but then it was their nightly ritual that she would finish...*

"Now I lay me down to sleep..." that was Bill's part. And Rachel sleepily took over, "I pray the Lord my soul to keep. If I should die before I wake, I pray the Lord my soul to take." And, as she named family and friends for God to bless, her back got scratched. Her eyes got heavy. She received her Dad's love, and she drifted off to sleep.

Bill sat for a long time in the dark still tickling her back listening to her deep slow breathing and thought, "There seems to be less and less that she wants to do with me. Teenage girls hanging out with their Dads? Well, what could we do together that she would enjoy and would be our special deal?"

And there it was, the idea. Just an answer to a little prayer...just like that...and the next miracle was that he pulled it off.

Several weeks later, on Christmas morning, Rachel opened an envelope from "Dad." It contained all the traveling and marketing information for three days of skiing for two in Keystone, Colorado. Her initial excitement about a big, "Out West" ski trip was tempered a little by the thought, "With my Dad? Just the two of us?"

Fast forward several more weeks, and they were on the plane, then on the slopes. They laughed and skied and chased each other all over the snow, "hoopin' and hollerin' and jumpin' and crashin' just wearing themselves out in the process." They were having a wonderful time!

The last night, Bill took Rachel to dinner up on the mountain. It was a thirty minute gondola ride to get to the scenic, mountaintop restaurant. They were both tired from three hard days of skiing, but they were hungry and the view at dusk was incredible. They were sharing fondue. "What is fondue?" Rachel had no clue. Bill had been talking about it since arriving in Keystone, but he wouldn't explain what it was. He had just said, "Wait and see. You'll like it."

And, she did. The whole evening could not have been more perfect for a Dad trying to love a daughter and hang on to that special place a Dad is supposed to have in his daughter's heart.

Having overeaten, they climbed back into the gondola, just the two of them. They were talked-out, laughed-out and skied-out. Tomorrow they would return to the "real world" of school and work, father-daughter tiffs and teenage attitudes, parental authority and the gradual tearing away from Mom and Dad that adolescence demands. But, tonight, it was cold and dark and peaceful. The stars were so bright just outside the gondola window. The extra blankets on the seat were not quite enough, so Rachel wrapped one around her as best she could. She allowed her Dad to put his warm arm around her and draw her close to him.

Soon, she was fast asleep in the gently swaying vessel that carried them the 30 minutes back toward home. Her head in his lap, his fingers gently touching her hair. In the peace of that moment, Bill sang "Fire and Rain" to his daughter and then ended with, "Now I lay me down to sleep…"

Two years later, Bill lost his beloved Rachel in a tragic car accident.

Value every moment, he would say. Value what really matters, for you never know when it may be taken away.

CHAPTER TWO

Realize That Things Are Not Always What They Seem!

"Your vision will become clear when you look into your heart".

Carl Jung
Author

Why is there Braille on the driver's side of an ATM?

Why are there interstate highways in Hawaii?

Who was the first person to look at a cow and say, "I think I will squeeze these dangly things here and drink whatever comes out?"

These questions bring a smile to your face, don't they? Makes you wonder what the people were thinking in each situation. There must be an acceptable explanation. Obviously, things are not always what they seem!

THE DENT

The successful, young executive had owned his fabulous new Mercedes for just a few weeks. His Chicago-based company had given him an early end to his Thursday afternoon, so he decided to take a short cut through one of the low-income areas that flank the city. His Michigan Avenue window office had seemed a bit stuffy on this gloriously sunny afternoon.

As he cruised through the rough neighborhood, he was oblivious to the shabby row houses and ghetto-like apartment buildings. Suddenly, he heard a thud on the passenger's side of his car. Slamming on the brakes, he could see a boy standing guiltily on the sidewalk behind him. He grabbed his cell phone and punched in 911 while he quickly backed up. He jumped out of the car and yelled at the boy. "What are you doing? You just trashed the side of my car," he said pointing to the large dent on the back door.

"Please sir. I am so sorry. I needed some help and no one would stop." Expecting to be jumped at any moment, the man looked all around for the rest of the gang. Nothing happened.

"My brother is over there, and he fell out of his old wheelchair. I can't get him up. Will you help me?"

"Sure," the executive thought. He had heard of traps to "roll" some ususpecting "patsy," but this was a new one.

The man looked behind the boy expecting to see his gang charging him with knives and guns. Instead, he saw another boy lying just behind the bushes. Still worrying about a trick, slowly and suspiciously, he walked toward the boy lying on the ground. There was the wheelchair, sideways in the grass. He gently lifted it to an upright position and whispered quietly. "I am sorry. I will help you."

As the boys rolled away, the young executive stared first at the twosome as they disappeared and then, at the dent in his car. He wiped the tears which were now streaming down his face and vowed never to have the dent fixed. It would be a constant reminder that he jumped to conclusions. "Never again!" he whispered as he climbed into his car.

> *"You never find yourself until you face the truth."*
> Pearl Bailey
> Entertainer

What would you have done had you come upon the same situation? Have the joys of the past kept you optimistic about people's motives and their capabilities? Or, do the transgressions of others deter your ability to love and accept those who would brighten your life?

Write down a situation where you jumped to conclusions. Now consider a time when you realized people or things were not what they had seemed at first glance.

A man walked into a car dealership with his toolbox in his hand. The salesman greeted him coolly and sent him to the back where the service department was located. The man walked out the back door and went to the dealership down the street where he paid cash for his new $40, 000 car. He paid for it with the money in his toolbox!

Often, it is our own interpretation of words that gets us into trouble. Try this little word game. Look at the word and decide what comes to mind when you see it. You will learn a lot about your psyche from what your first response is...

ADD

Adding or attention deficit disorder?

BEAR or BARE

Did you think of an animal or someone undressed?

BEETLE or BEATLE

The bug or a rock group?

FIRE

Something burning or losing your job?

FLAG

Someone trying to stop passing cars or "Old Glory?"

GOD

An exclamatory reaction or the power that rules your life?

HERO

Superman or fireman raising a flag over ground zero?

PLUS

An addition problem or a size 14 woman?

TRAFFIC

Construction or the movie about drugs starring Michael Douglas?

It's amazing how words and our interpretation of them mold our attitudes and our perceptions. This little game can become a survey of your thoughts if you choose to conceive of more words. You will find that often reality is colored by the definition we give the words we hear.

This is the ultimate of paradoxes. When people judge by what they see or hear, reputations are ruined, lives changed. Things are not always what they seem.

History shares reminders for future generations about looking past the obvious to the reality. Consider the story of one elderly couple decades ago.

The old couple knocked softly on the President of Harvard University's huge wooden door. As they entered his imposing office, the university's leader stared at the old couple with utter disbelief. They were disheveled and bent over as they shyly entered the room. He looked at his watch wondering why his secretary had allowed this appointment.

"Our son was a student here at Harvard, and he loved it," the old man said. Pausing and staring at his distraught wife, he continued, "You see, he died several months ago, and we want to do something here in his honor. We want to give money to have a building named after him."

Staring at their old clothes and resenting the fact that this less than impressive couple had interrupted his busy schedule, the President almost laughed out loud. Then, he proceeded to bluntly explain how it cost a great deal of money, and they couldn't possibly afford a building... maybe a plaque on some pre-existing door.

When the old man began to restate his case, the President rose and ushered the couple out of his office. The woman looked sadly at her husband as they shuffled away. As he hurriedly shut the door, the President heard the old man say, "Please don't be sad. It doesn't matter. We will find some land and build our own university." The President could not restrain himself any longer and erupted into laughter.

The year was 1884...the old man was Leland Stanford. His son had died of typhoid fever several months before. The old man bought his land and with the money he had made from building the Central Pacific Railroad, he founded Stanford University to honor his son!

And, then, there were the "rag-tag" twelve following an unknown carpenter turned preacher. Most were poor and uneducated. Yet, they made sure the words taught by their master would forever change the course of history. Can you imagine how many people dismissed these men as unimpressive if not down-right crazy? Can you imagine how many never accepted the fact that things were definitely not what they appeared to be in that group?

Have you been guilty of judging by looks or dress? Have you ever been the victim of such superficial opinions? Jot down some ways you have felt in each situation.

In life, we have opportunities each day to face the ramifications of our judgment.

How deeply do you look at the results of your actions?

Do you choose your friends by what is on the outside or what is deep inside?

Have you ever wondered about what kind of person would want to be a reporter? After all, they have to snoop around and ask insensitive questions, right? They are all looking for a story that will win them a Pulitzer Prize, aren't they? After more than twenty years of working with the media, I contend that this one particular profession epitomizes the essence of the "things are not always what they seem" concept.

Reporters are students. That's right! Reporters are students. Their job is to learn everything they can, as quickly as they can about an assigned subject. And, like classroom students, they all learn at their own pace, with their own means of remembering and with their own preconceived notions about the subject. Think about it! Isn't that true?

How often do you sit in a quandary in front of a TV screen because some reporter doesn't seem to understand the subject he's sharing with you? When was the last time you read a story and wondered where this guy had gotten his information? Who was his teacher? Did the source find clear ways of relaying the truth so that you weren't ready to shoot the "messenger?" Remember, that's what a reporter should be...a good learner who is the deliverer of a clear, unbiased message. He cannot jump to conclusions without destroying his credibility.

> *"Reputation is what people think about you. Character is what people know you are!"*
>
> Anonymous

When I teach media relations, the first thing I do is attempt to dispel common misconceptions about reporters. They are real people with families and children and avocations and goals and, in most cases, deep moral convictions that are challenged on a fairly regular basis. "What you see" in the media is not necessarily always what it may seem.

As a real test of your ability to discriminate between what is fact and what is not...remembering that things are not always what they seem...try this self-test the next time you watch TV and again as you read your next news story.

Who was the source for the story?

What was the agenda of the source?

What kind of learner was the reporter based on how he interpreted the facts?

How was the story positioned in the newscast and in the paper? Placement is a key to discerned importance.

When did the story run...immediately after the occurrence, days later, maybe weeks?

Are they doing their job diligently and professionally? Is their story solid?

If you are a school teacher like me, you never really lose your ability to evaluate the people who are learning from you. Remember, reporters are students willing and anxious to learn. They may not be what they seem in the glare of the camera.

Like reporters, single people are on a journey for information. I bet you thought they were just looking for companionship. In reality, they are learning about themselves and about those they meet.

Sadly, in the world of dating, things are not always what they seem. Today, so many men and women, particularly in the 50+ category, are playing games. If you don't know or understand the rules of the game, you WILL lose. The first and probably most important rule is things are not always what they seem! Some people will say and be whatever they believe keeps them in the game. That may mean lying about jobs, activities, religion, finances and oh, so prevalent, their marital status.

Many singles are not really liars. If asked, they would probably answer truthfully, but sadly most people, no matter what their age, don't ask key questions. Maybe they really do not want to know, because the answers may confuse the search for "love."

Imagine what the world would be like if everyone told the truth. And people were recognized only for their honesty. It is regrettable that society has elevated lying to such an art form. Look

at some of the reality television shows like Survivor or The Bachelor. The winners are those who can fool the other players or hide some elements of the truth. It often seems that "fudging" is expected in today's society. I contend that nothing is more damaging in a relationship than lying. People presenting things contrary to the truth are one of the key elements behind our country's skepticism, pessimism and negativism.

Think of this the next time you meet someone new or approach your work day. You will not regret telling the truth.

A SHELL IS NOT A SHELL AT ALL

Today, as I walked on the beach, I had no intention of looking for shells. I was just strolling for no particular reason. Then, a small shell caught my eye.

I don't know why...it was glistening in the sun amidst millions of others, but it looked just like what I wanted. So, I bent down and picked it up. As I walked on, I saw other shells that seemed interesting to me, so I picked them up, too. In all, I returned home with at least thirty unique new pieces to my life.

Why were these particular shells the ones I wanted? I still didn't know. Maybe it was their color or texture or their shapes. Something about them made me want to get to know them better.

Oh, there were others that I saw. Some I walked right by and never gave a second thought. Some caused me to pause and maybe even bend down to see them more closely, but then, I would move on. I picked up some shells, but saw they were flawed with cracks, or they had "stuff" in them that I didn't want to have to deal with. So, I threw them back to the sea.

As I looked at the shells in my hand, I realized none were exactly alike. I had chosen them without forethought or analysis. I just liked them and knew they would brighten my life.

Isn't that what life is like? We see people. People see us. We choose people, and we don't know why. People choose us, and they aren't sure why. Do our first impressions rob us of new experiences?

We accept, and we reject. We are accepted, and we are rejected. Why?

We are each unique, and, if we are truly blessed, we are found to be unique by those who see us or touch our lives.

Some people we take home; some we only look at and move on.

Some will take us into their lives; some will pick us up, and then throw us back to the world.

Some will just love us for what we are and then, they will take us home.

Some we will love and bring into our hearts.

Will we find they were not what we had at first thought they were?

Are they filled with "goop" we can't handle? Do they bear scars we can't explain and didn't initially see?

When we find just the right "shells" for us, what do we do with them?

Do we take them home and clean them up? Do we put them in a precious spot in our lives? Or, do we admire them for a while, then put them in a box or a drawer only to be brought out on a whim?

And, how are we treated when chosen from the beach and taken home?

Do people jump to conclusions about our worth or our ability to satisfy?

Do those who choose us want to accept us as we are or do they want to change us?

Are we pampered and cared for and put in a special place to be seen daily? Or, are we broken and cracked from years of carelessness or being shoved in a back room?

Are we ignored because it takes too much time and effort to see us for who we really are and not what people expected us to be?

No matter what the answers, we are all special!

Those we picked so carefully off of life's beach were chosen and brought a long way from the crashing waves into the safety of our lives.

We chose them for a reason, and they chose us. We must never forget. We must never lose them for they were the ones we picked and, we were the ones they picked!

Isn't life special? Even shells are not what they seem!

Several years ago, a Louisville, Kentucky radio station decided to do a series about the homeless before Christmas. It was prompted by a caller asking why he "should help these guys. They should just find a job and become model citizens." A young reporter ventured out to find out who would live without a home. She was astonished at what she discovered and so were her listeners.

One man was a PhD who had succumbed to alcoholism. His affluent life style had disappeared as quickly as the bottles of bourbon he had consumed. With the help of a shelter and friends who searched tirelessly to find out where he had vanished, the man was destined to turn his life around. Another man was a talented musician. He actually sang original music for the young reporter's story. He had lost his home because he had fallen for a scam to get his songs recorded. He, too, was articulate and gifted. A third person was a woman whose divorce had left her penniless and without a home. Because she had only a high school education, she knew she would have to look for menial work at entry levels. She wasn't a loser mooching off of the government as referred to by many critics of the homeless. She was a woman with no family to help her, no resources to fall back on, and no means of income. However, she was articulate and street-wise. She had survived alone since she was a teenager, and she had chosen to seek help from local volunteers to prepare her for a job.

Often, all these people would be ignored, misjudged and deemed as useless, when they are actually of great value and because some people chose to believe that things are not always what they seem, they will be homeless no more.

Martin Luther King said, "It is not the color of your skin, but the content of your character that determines who you are."

> *"Let one therefore keep the mind pure, for what a man thinks, that he becomes."*
>
> The Upanishads
> Hindu Philosophy

Jesus said, "Judge not, that ye be not judged."

The next time you attend an event or sit at a restaurant, look around you, not just at the patrons, but at the staff. Study their demeanor. Learn from their responses...not just from what you see.

Consider four year old Mary Beth who proudly faced her Sunday school teacher and proclaimed, "I know my older sister loves me, because she gives me all her old clothes. Then, she HAS to go buy new ones!"

Things are not always what they seem. Look at the following candidates for world leader. Who would you vote for?

Candidate A----associates with crooked politicians, consults with astrologists, has had two mistresses, chain smokes and drinks eight to ten martinis a day.

Candidate B----was kicked out of office twice, sleeps until noon, used opium in college and drinks a quart of whiskey every evening.

Candidate C----is a decorated war hero, a vegetarian, doesn't smoke, drinks an occasional beer and hasn't had any extramarital affairs.

Which of these candidates would make the best world leader?

If you voted for Candidate A, you elected Franklin D. Roosevelt.

If you voted for Candidate B, you elected Winston Churchill.

If you voted for Candidate C, you elected Adolf Hitler.

History again is a great teacher.

And one final little quiz before we wind up CHAPTER TWO of *The Magnificent Seven Plus ONE*. It is a moral dilemma...

If you knew a woman who was pregnant and already had eight kids...three who were deaf, two who were blind, one mentally retarded and the mother has syphilis...would you recommend that she have an abortion? Would you recommend an abortion even if you are the most adamant anti-abortionist? Quite a thought! The answer seems so obvious, yet if you said yes to the abortion, you have just killed Beethoven.

Are you surprised at the results of these quizzes? Do you think you are intuitive about those around you and assess situations only after you have gathered adequate information? Are you what the Myers-Briggs (a well-known management test used for evaluating business communication styles), calls "Introspective"...assessing all aspects and being open-minded or are you "Judging," which will make you more often a person who forgets that things are not always what they seem.

This man was so busy. He had a deadline to get THE boat finished, and he was working feverishly day and night. He enlisted the aid of his sons and daughters while the neighbors scoffed at his endeavors. After all, why in the world did Noah need an ark in the middle of the desert? "By faith, Noah built a ship in the middle of the dry land. He was warned about something he couldn't see and acted on what he was told..." (Old Testament). A crazy man performing a seemingly ridiculous task. The outcome proved things were not what they seemed.

An old woman died in a geriatric ward in Ireland several years ago. Among her meager possessions was a poem she had written. It was circulated among the nurses there and later published in the Ireland Mental Health Associations' *News Magazine of the North*.

What do you see, nurse, what do you see?
What are you thinking when you're looking at me?
A crabby old woman, not very wise,
Uncertain of habit, with faraway eyes?
Who dribbles her food and makes no reply
When you say in a loud voice, "I do wish you'd try!"
Who seems not to notice the things that you do,
And forever is losing a stocking or shoe...
Who, resisting or not, lets you do as you will,
With bathing and feeding, the long day to fill...
Is that what you are thinking? Is that what you see?
Then open your eyes, nurse; you're not looking at me.
I'll tell you who I am as I sit here so still,
As I do at your bidding, as I eat at your will.
I'm a small child of ten...with a father and mother,

Brothers and sisters, who love one another.
A young girl of sixteen, with wings on her feet,
Dreaming that soon now her lover she'll meet.
A bride soon at twenty...my heart gives a leap,
Remembering the vows that I promised to keep.
At twenty-five now, I have young of my own,
Who need a guide and a secure, happy home.
A woman of thirty, my young now grown fast,
Bound to each other with ties that should last.
At forty, my young sons have grown and are gone,
But, my man's beside me to see I don't mourn.
At fifty once more, babies play around my knee,
Again we know children, my loved one and me,
Dark days are upon me. My husband is dead!
I look at the future; I shudder with dread.
For my young are all rearing young of their own,
And I think of the years and the love I have known.
I'm now an old woman...and nature is cruel.
'Tis jest to make old age look like a fool!
The body it crumbles, grace and vigor depart,
There is now a stone where I once had a heart.
But inside this old carcass, a young girl still dwells,
And now and again, my battered heart swells.
I remember the joys, I remember the pain,
And I am loving and living life over again.
I think of the years...all too few, gone too fast,
And accept the stark fact that nothing can last!
So open your eyes, nurses, open and see...
Not a crabby old woman. Look closer...SEE ME!

Remember this poem at the very instant you begin to judge
someone next time! Things are not always what they seem!

CHAPTER THREE

Take Care Of Yourself...
Be Your Own Best Caregiver!

"The outside world mirrors what is in you!
You are seen as you see yourself."

Barbara Streisand
Singer / Actress

> *"Self-discipline is self-caring."*
>
> *M. Scott Peck*
> *Author*

Of course, we are all different, and we are all gifted in a variety of ways. Really taking care of ourselves means knowing ourselves, loving ourselves, forgiving ourselves and laughing at ourselves.

Here we go! Everybody is talking about taking care of yourself. Dr. Phil wants you to change how you eat. Tony Little wants you to buy his exercise equipment. Yoga experts want you to meditate. Consultants want you to hire them. Closet organizers want you to get your storage space cleaned up because that surely gives you the peace of mind you need to take care of yourself.

Did you know that the two most popular books purchased in book stores are cookbooks and diet books? What does that mean?

I have another thought. Get rid of some things in your life that keep you segregated from the relationships that matter. How many televisions do you have in your home? How many telephones? How many cell, land, work, and computer lines?

When you chose this book, what were you looking for? Was it an easy fix to a complicated life? Taking care of your mental, emotional and spiritual self is the key. The physical will come as you rid yourself of the unnecessary and find time for the essential.

And who determines what is important to you? That's the biggest question to think about. Who is that person? Your boss, your spouse, your children…you? Think long and hard about that, because the answer will be the key to taking care of yourself.

How strong are your needs? On a scale of one to ten, one being a low need, answer the following…

How important is it to you to be the center of attention?

To be on stage?

To be patted on the back for a job well done?

To be told you are loved?

The degree with which we need this kind of recognition has a great deal to do with our happiness, our stress, disappointment levels and our success. We have to know where we are on this scale before we can really take care of ourselves.

My husband, who needs virtually no compliments, fears being on stage or in the limelight and never seeks an opportunity to be the center of attention. On a scale of ten, his levels of need are probably about a three. He is an extremely successful entrepreneur and CEO of a $24,000,000 company, but he breaks into a cold sweat if he has to speak in front of people.

I, on the other end of the spectrum, am about a nine on the attention needs scale. I love compliments, and I seek opportunities to be on the proverbial and literal stage. My husband thinks there is something wrong with me. On the other hand, I think he is just plain strange.

Aren't we the epitome of opposites attracting? Does it equate that successful people have lower attention needs...NO! Look at the world around you. Look at YOUR world. Are you in a place where people give you the level of recognition or attention that keeps you fulfilled and confident? Ponder that for a while. Maybe that is why we do not take time enough for ourselves. Could it be that we are so busy looking for positive feedback that we run from project to project and say yes when we really do not have the time for more commitments? "Whirling dervishes" seldom find the warmth of sitting quietly to appreciate a sunset. A computer is worthless if ideas are thrown onto the screen without ever being named or saved. We become forgetful, because we are so busy that we don't hit the "save" button on our "mental computers."

Consider the thousands of single people in this world. They anxiously seek reassurance of their worth in the eyes of strangers. Those with high "need" scales don't care who compliments them or where they have to go to get self-gratification. They just have to be "gushed over!" Without this attention, no matter how hollow the words, these people are restless, angry and often, depressed.

Naturally, compliments make us all feel loved and important. The way they are packaged and the motives that inspire their utterance in the first place help us determine their sincerity.

Could you be your own best source of inspiration?

Can you take care to scrutinize what is real and what is meant to be a superficial comment?

Can you find value in yourself when you look in the mirror or does it take the words of someone else to make you feel special?

I contend that if you do not think you are special, then very few others will think that you are. There are ways to find this inner comfort. The first and I think the most important is to take time for your spiritual self. After all, Moses and Jesus disappeared for forty days to commune with God and find the strength to change the world. How about finding time for your own life changing growth?

I urge you to come to a quiet place daily where you can delve into your spiritual self. There is so much you can do for yourself here if only you are listening. If you commit to discovering your inspiration from within, you will observe all around you what strengthens and refreshes your spirit. Try the following techniques to ensure that you will enhance your relationship with your God.

SPIRITUAL PRACTICE STEPS

FIND A SACRED SPACE

COMMIT TO A DAILY SPIRITUAL PRACTICE

FOCUS ON THE LITTLE THINGS

INDULGE IN ACTIVITIES THAT FEED YOUR SOUL

CREATE AMAZING MOMENTS

PLAN A REGULAR "RETREAT FOR YOUR SOUL"

Here is a rather elementary exercise that you can use to build your self confidence. Each morning for two weeks as you face yourself in the mirror, say, "I am a special person who is an important part of this world!" I know what you are thinking. "I am not going to do that. My family or my roommate or my spouse or my kids will laugh me right out of the house." Some of us already build ourselves up as we begin our days, but maybe not in those exact same words. Think about it. How do you launch yourself into the rigors of your day? Surely you whisper some secret words of encouragement or prayers of guidance. However you choose to take care of your confidence level, be sure to start your morning with God along with a compliment to yourself.

Now that your day has begun, how scattered are you? What chances for fulfilling your needs are you missing because you race from one thing to another without seeing the opportunities? In a nutshell, taking care of yourself requires daily moments of reflection on what you have learned and experienced. Be sure you recognize your feelings and responses to all that you have seen and done.

Lest you think I am telling you that being self-centered is the best way to be your own best caregiver, let me show you the other side of the coin.

Giving to others will always be an essential part of taking care of yourself. Those who have no time for helping a stranger...notice I did not say money, I said TIME...those people will never feel completely good about themselves. We are programmed to give unselfishly. At what levels and for what reasons are the variables, but without this commitment to volunteerism, there can be no completely successful life. I would not presume to tell you where to volunteer or how many times to include such in your schedule. I just encourage you to have a cause and support it passionately.

Take the space below to write where your interests lie. Think of friends or family and what may have happened in their lives. Look at yourself. Where are your talents, where has there been a challenge in your life? What gets you excited and ideas flowing?

Next, think of the non-profit organizations in your area. List the ones that fit your experiences, your talents and your interests.

Now dive into that volunteer project! Careful…only one or two, because even in valuable deeds, spreading yourself too thin will sabotage your commitment to take care of yourself.

YOUR ROLE IN THE LIVES OF OTHERS

Close your eyes and see a world different from your own.

The beautiful American movie star leaned down to touch the tiny child. His stomach bloated from malnutrition and his little brown eyes bulging from their sockets. Tears filled the woman's eyes as she cradled the child hoping to have him eat. Can you see them sitting amidst the squalor of a refugee camp in some unknown country?

Look in another direction…See the man shivering in the cold. He lies in a box that once protected a new refrigerator. The fingers of his gloves are worn and his knuckles are blue from the cold. The railroad tracks just over his head rattle and rumble with the sound of another train. He closes his eyes and moans. Quietly, a man leans over and covers him with one…no…two blankets. The homeless man opens his eyes and attempts to smile. He sees food in the stranger's hand. He reaches for the spoon and downs it quickly.

"The only ones among you who will be really happy are those who will have sought and found how to serve."

Albert Schweitzer
Missionary Physician,
Philosopher

Now look over there, just behind you. The mother cradles her child, but there are tears rolling down her cheeks. She enters the Children's Hospital. A lady in pink walks up to her and asks if she needs anything while she waits for the results of her baby's test. The woman smiles at the mother then lightly touches her hand. "It will be all right. They do great things here!"

Can you see them…those who give of themselves?

Rick Warren author of *The Purpose Driven Life* would say that these people have forgotten themselves long enough to lend a helping hand. Imagine a world with no one helping others. No blood drives, no food pantries, no clothing donations, no homeless shelters, no Girl or Boy Scout troops, no leadership programs, no Synagogue or church classes, no Young Life, no Little League or soccer, nothing that requires giving without being paid.

What would you be missing in your own life?

Will you share what you know and love with groups that need it?

What rewards do YOU need to give of yourself?

If there were no volunteers in your life, what would you have to give up?

Think about that!

Imagine if you were the little child or the homeless man or the mother with the sick baby and no one reached out to you.

Why do people give of themselves?

Paul, once a Roman who persecuted believers of Christ, was transformed on the road to Damascus. He became a believer in Christ and was himself persecuted for his commitment. He wrote to his friends in Corinth nearly 2000 years ago, "Those in frequent contact with the things of the world should make good use of them without becoming attached to them…"

Here is what many people give as their reasons for volunteering...

MOST OBVIOUS -- To help others

It makes me feel good

To be in the limelight

For my own glory

Because my boss or my teacher said I couldn't succeed if I didn't

To pay somebody back for helping me

To look good

Because I can meet that girl I saw yesterday

Because my family gave me a legacy of volunteerism

Because I believe God expects me to!

Some of these reasons sound familiar? Did I forget any? Why do you work for nothing? That's what it is, you know. You are working for nothing...OR ARE YOU???

Woody Hayes, the great Ohio State University football coach, always said you should "pay forward"...pay before you earn. How does that feel to you? What are the rewards of giving? Do you know how to volunteer?

You must know yourself first...what gifts do you have? Are you artistic? Do you like to sing...do you love animals...do you love collecting money...do you like to see children smile or hear stories from people who've seen so much... do you like to teach what you know...are you a computer whiz? Do you have clothes you have outgrown or games you are tired of? Have you lost someone and you know how it feels to be sad? Just look how you can impact the lives of strangers!

The time to volunteer is a combination of when volunteerism is needed and when YOU have fulfilled your own commitments. Most organizations will be delighted to fit your efforts into their agenda at your convenience. Remember, to really take care of yourself, you must cultivate your special gifts and share them with others.

WHAT WILL BE YOUR GIFT?

How much does a hug cost?

How hard is a car wash?

What reward a bag of grocery things?

What gift an old jacket brings?

How special a child's bright smile?

How priceless to talk for awhile?

These are the moments of giving

That bring real meaning to living.

Without these ANGELS, there

Would be no spark.

Without them, there would be

A world with no real heart!!

Using your assets has become such a standard theme in today's business arena. Taking care of yourself requires that you utilize your skills, your talents, your experiences and your assets. Call these qualities what you like, but remember, you will never feel truly satisfied until you are doing what you do best. A wise woman once asked, "How many people do what they want without concern for money? When one achieves this balance, work isn't work...it's love!"

We've all heard the horror stories of the great salesman who is rewarded for his efforts by a promotion to sales manager, and he fails miserably. He loved to sell...he did not love to manage people. It happens all the time as bosses try to find the right way to reward a successful employee. Bosses too often think a promotion to a different job with higher salary is the reward that works for the employee and fits the company structure. But, has anyone really focused on finding the special gifts in the employee then finding the job that will ensure success? Not often enough!

As part of taking care of yourself, you must not only know what your special gifts are, you must capitalize on them. How simple does that sound?

Since the age of thirteen, I have been an avid golfer. My talented mother who had been club champion for two different country clubs taught me this wonderful game. It gave me the chance to share not only time but a lifelong passion with her. I discovered my love of competition and my attention to detail through the years of playing. I worked hard to excel at golf in high school and have continued to hone my skills ever since. Unfortunately, I will never be as good as I would like, but I love the self-nurturing the sport still brings me today.

Many years ago, I began watching golf on television, because I just knew I would learn some secret that would move my handicap to a single digit...for you non-golfers that's golf lingo for really good. I found myself following a flamboyant, quite handsome touring professional named Payne Stewart. He was colorful and joyous about this game of golf. He brought laughter and enthusiasm to a sport once considered only for the "stuffy affluent." I remember when Payne won the US Open by sinking a seemingly impossible putt to beat Phil Mickelson. Instead of shaking Phil's hand, Payne hugged his opponent and whispered in his ear, "You are about to be a father. That is the greatest prize of all." At that moment, golf transcended the world of sport and became an impetus to greatness.

Less than a year later, Payne Stewart and his friends stepped onto a small jet and ascended into the spectacular blue sky over Florida. God must be a golfer, because on that day, Payne kept rising to heaven never to return again. All who knew him and loved Payne believed God must have needed a fourth for golf that day.

Recently, I met a dear friend of Payne's and a great golfer in his own right...Peter Jacobsen, who has won many times on the PGA Tour and has just joined the Senior tour. He represents the joy, skill and passion that makes golf more than just a game.

Where is your passion? If you don't have a sport where you can release your inhibitions, stretch your muscles and expand your mind, please find one! Don't you think Jesus and the disciples might have fished for fun, not just for food? If you love the water, why not take up kayaking or swimming? If you have a passion to whack something, take up tennis or racquetball or handball? If you love the cold, get out to that rink or strap on those skis. If you would rather be warmer, get a bike or running shoes or a softball bat.

Whatever you choose, just get out there and enjoy this great world that has been entrusted to us. Your mind will be refreshed even more than your body!

Finding the right sport is just like any other endeavor in your life. You have to know your capabilities and your limitations. Shouldn't we capitalize on our assets then stretch the boundaries of our experiences? We grow by letting ourselves stretch to try something new. It may only be for an avocation and/or for a one-time lark. But, what pleasure comes from such a physical AND mental adventure!

Try this ...

Jot down a skill that you have. Try to think of something removed from your job or your daily activities. Something you have always wanted to do but never really tried. Now, arrange to do it!

Think of something you did as a child that you loved. Maybe it was camping or horseback riding or ballet. Go do it again. Then, ask yourself how you feel afterwards. Are you renewed, excited, childlike?

Do you feel like you did when you first experienced this adventure? Are memories welling up inside you that delight and titillate you? What a great feeling.

In 2001, I took an unofficial survey of friends and acquaintances from all over the world. I had met them during my annual trips to fabulous Marco Island, Florida and had known them in Columbus, Ohio or Louisville, Kentucky. I asked them to think back on their childhood and remember the games they played, and the expectations they had for their futures. (You will get a chance to take this quiz in Chapter Five.) The outcome of this exercise was enlightening and frankly, really great fun for those who participated. I discovered aspiring June Taylor dancers, star football players, talented seamstresses, gifted pianists, even budding poets. I was curious as to how many of these talents had been cultivated and were still filling their lives. Sadly, more than half had not pursued their gifts. Some even noted the regret that they were not now involved in the passions of their youth at all.

I had to ask, "What is wrong with reinstating that past love into your present and your future?" Some laughed and said, "I'm too old!" "Never too old!" I retorted. Others grinned and closed their eyes deep in thought. Still others vowed to get right back into their various childhood passions.

Taking care of you means allowing yourself the indulgence of pursuing your own interests, hobbies and talents. What are yours? Remember, you will never find your special gifts if you don't stretch your memory to retry something old or indulge your imagination to adventurously try something new.

You're reading this saying, "How can I possibly take on anything else in my life? I am already so overwhelmed with my commitments and my responsibilities." I contend that we get that drowning feeling when we are doing things that we are (a) not very astute at doing or (b) not excited about. Isn't that true? If you are dead tired and someone calls to ask if you'd like to go to dinner or a movie or better still, plan a weekend getaway, what happens to your energy level? Suddenly, you are excited and "fired-up." Why not keep up that euphoric feeling all the time by focusing on what gives you spiritual energy?

But what about that "time" thing? How can we take care of ourselves with all those responsibilities and commitments? Here are a few ideas...

Write down all the things you are involved in. (There are blank pages at the end of the book for this exercise.) Besides your work-related responsibilities, be sure to include the children's activities, your workout routine, cleaning the house and shopping for groceries. Everything. Put them down the left side of the page and across the top make three columns entitled...

DO IT   HIRE IT   DUMP IT

Put check marks beside each activity under the appropriate column.

This is the hard part...deciding how you will actually handle the responsibilities. If you have all of the checks under the first column the DO IT column...you had better reevaluate. The greatest failures in life are those who try to do it all. So, give it up!

Now, back to the chart. We all understand the concept of DO IT and there truly are things that ONLY YOU can do...but, don't let your ego take over or allow your desire to control take control of you. Give up some things to the HIRE IT or DUMP IT column. One quick hint...hiring doesn't necessarily require paying for services. Remember bartering? It was once the economic foundation of the world. And, when you exchange something you need, why not offer something you love to do. Consider the executive woman who needs the interior of her house painted but has no time or skill to do it herself. She knows of a single mother who needs childcare. The women negotiate the exchange of services and for the busy executive, the chance to enjoy children is a refreshing change for her. She is excited to play the role of "aunt" so the time doesn't matter. Or how about the guy who knows the lawn needs care, but when? What if he offered his box seats at an upcoming hockey game to the neighbor's teenager in exchange for the services? No more pressure for the project, more time that would have been lost at the game, no money changes hands, everybody wins! Sound bizarre? Well, it works. Look at your list and think outside the box. Or, just spend the money to HAVE the jobs done that weigh so heavily on your mind AND your agenda.

What is your dilemma? Do you like the first idea of just doing it and you feel that you might try the second one if only you could just find the right person to delegate it to? But you have a real problem with the third one. DUMP IT!!! "You have got to be kidding, right?" you exclaim! "There's nothing I am doing now that I could let go of. I mean the Cancer Society Board really needs me. My daughter's teacher wants me to help in the classroom. My assistant asked me to show her more about the new computer system. I'm the only one that can do that. They want me to drive the carpool three weeks in a row while Susan is recovering from her surgery. My boss suggested I work out with him three days a week at his health club across town even though I have my own club I attend regularly."

I would imagine you have made similar statements just in the last few days. From the outside, nearly all of these time commitments look easy to DUMP. If you owned them could you say "NO?" Would you say "NO?" Is it our egos that keep us saying "YES" when our minds and sometimes our fatigued bodies shout "SAY NO?" When will we find time to take care of ourselves if we don't learn to back off from some of the commitments that are not really on the track we hope to be traveling on?

Look at your list again and circle the things that you are doing which really have no relationship to your goals and your commitments. They are things you do as a favor to a friend or as payback for help you have received or even to get your photo in the paper. Is the stress of fulfilling the obligation overshadowing the rewards? If so, check it off in the DUMP IT column.

How do you feel? Relieved, guilty, confused, excited for the time to do what fulfills you. And, don't regress when someone panics that you are saying no. They will get over it. They've heard it before, just not from you. Isn't it fun to surprise people?

Remember…DO IT! HIRE IT! DUMP IT! Your new management technique.

Worry is interest paid in trouble before it is due. Worry wears us down to the point we cannot face daily responsibilities, much less our futures. The best remedy for worrying is planning.

A LIFE PLAN

Robin Norwood, author, has written, "We achieve a sense of self from what we do for ourselves and how we develop our capacities. If all your efforts have gone into developing others, you're bound to feel empty. TAKE YOUR TURN NOW!"

Look at your life's plan…do you even have a plan? Taking care of yourself means you have a plan just like the vision or mission statements that guide businesses of all sizes. What is your vision for your life? Do you see yourself married, a parent, a corporate leader, an Olympic Gold medalist, an award-winning artist, a relaxed thinker? What is your mission? Do you want to share your faith, help people, invent something, win an award, improve someone's life, change the course of history or just love and be loved? What is your final destination?

On a brightly colored sheet of paper, write YOUR VISION and MISSION.

Hang it near you at work and at home. That's what companies do. In fact, I remember spending months developing just the perfect verbiage at a hospital corporation so that all who saw it would be inspired, challenged and encouraged by the words. You will be stronger and more committed just like the big corporations who post their vision and mission statements.

Now, one final thought as you consider taking care of yourself and it being the

"We are what we repeatedly do. Excellence, then is not an act, but a habit."

Aristotle
Greek Philosopher

third of the *Magnificent Seven Plus ONE.* You must be healthy. I used to laugh at the old attage, "If you have your health, you have everything." Now that I am over fifty and see people around me struggling with simple backaches all the way to cancer, strokes and heart attacks, I realize how true the statement is. Nothing else matters if you can't participate in life! You don't need another diet book or good health lecture to emphasize this truth. You are surrounded by thousands of self-help books on physical well-being. What you need is honest introspection. Try answering the following questions with candor...

How well do you sleep and why?

What do you eat and when?

How often do you exercise and how much of it is aerobic?

How often do you sit quietly and do absolutely nothing?

What are your special talents and how often do you put them to use?

Do you have a spiritual foundation from which you can draw strength whenever you are in need?

Are you overwhelmed with these questions? Don't be. They are meant to give you focus and to make you consider what you are doing for yourself.

So, will you take care of yourself?

CHAPTER FOUR
Know Who You Are...
Then Believe!

"The moment you doubt whether you can fly,
you cease forever to be able to do it. The reason
birds can fly, and we can't is simply that they
have perfect faith...for to have faith, is to have wings."

J.M. Barrie
Author of Peter Pan

Know Who You Are...Then Believe!

Are you flying yet? Now that you have taken care of yourself or at least you have read ideas that you have great intentions to adapt for yourself, remember that you are on a quest to be the best that you can be.

Look around you. Do you see people who seem to be accomplishing great things? You aren't quite sure what is different about them. They are constantly positive about their work or their friends or even their home. They always see the glass half full and not half empty. They do not seem to have problems circling around them like sharks. They can't be for real, you say. Nobody goes through life like this. And, maybe you are right. But, I bet they have simply decided to face life with a positive attitude. They pick and choose what will affect their reaction to their surroundings. Could it be they believe in focusing heavenward? Paul did. "Whatever you do, work at it with all your heart as working for the Lord, not for men!"

A very wise doctor once told me that others do not force us to do something no matter how unexpected the situation. We must accept responsibility for our actions and not say childishly, "They made me retaliate because they initially hurt me." That is an excuse...you must believe that your response to the unexpected is always your own choice.

By now, you have probably heard the true story of a young man with failing grades and minimal athletic ability who was told by everyone that his dream to play football for Notre Dame was absolutely ridiculous. A very successful movie called *Rudy* was released about him. But, the young man, Rudy, did play football and in the process proved for the thousandth time in history that believing in ourselves overcomes all barriers.

> *"This above all, to thine own self be true."*
> *William Shakespeare*
> *English Dramatist*

He was too little and too slow to be any good, but something inside of him drove him to be a part of the team. He decided he would play football at Notre Dame while his high school teachers, friends and even family laughed. What made Rudy ignore all those who dissuaded him? Was it the death of the one friend who believed in him or was it self-preservation? If you haven't seen the movie of this true story, I urge you to rent it...or better still, buy it and study it! The simple fact that Rudy knew who he was, then believed in himself, ensured he would reach his goal of playing at Notre Dame because his heart fit his attitude of success. Against all odds, he was a winner.

Let's look at another true story that has become a metaphor for the little man, *Seabiscuit*. You know the story of that nobody horse with a loser jockey and a trainer with little or no social skills and even less "book-learning." One man brought them together. He saw in each of them...the horse, the jockey and the trainer...a staunch self-confidence, but even more importantly, a will to succeed that even they couldn't fight. And, WIN they did! The irony is the men had to believe in themselves before they could ensure the success of their ironically successful horse.

And then, there is the paradox of one of the greatest minds of the twentieth century. Albert Einstein did not speak until he was four years old and didn't read until he was seven. His teachers described him as "mentally slow, unsociable and adrift forever in his foolish dreams." He was refused admittance to the Zurich Polytechnic Institute. Yet, he was one of the men who changed the course of human history. "I never came upon any of my discoveries through the process of rational thinking," declared Mr. Einstein.

When my father knocked on Einstein's door at Princeton University one warm afternoon in 1942, Einstein answered in a bathrobe with his usual rumpled hair. My father will never forget spending an hour in this amazing man's presence. Now, at 78, Dad still ponders the impact this one meeting had on his life.

Need one more? How about Walt Disney? He was nearly fired from several jobs because he showed no imagination or creativity. He almost went bankrupt before opening Disneyland. How many Disney movies have you seen in your lifetime? When was the last time you saw Mickey Mouse?

"To love oneself is the beginning of a lifelong romance."

Oscar Wilde
Playwright

Where is your confidence? Do you believe in yourself? Do you stay strong when those around you either ignore your seemingly unrealistic goals or ridicule you for setting your sights on something they can never see you achieving?

Know Who You Are...Then Believe!

When you were a kid, did you let what your family, teachers or friends said to you or about you influence your choices? Of course, you were a child then. You, I should say we, have matured and never make decisions or choices based on the impressions of co-workers, family or friends. Right? Ask yourself "Upon what did I base my last major decision?"

Eleanor Roosevelt, former First Lady, said, "No one can make you feel inferior without your permission."

I know a young woman who wanted to be a nurse. Stacey was told by more than one educator that she would never make it. Why? Because she was a terrible test-taker. Never mind that they conceded she had great bedside manner and even better empathy for her patients. She should have given up when she was told that there was no chance she would make it. She fought for her chance to grasp her dream. She knew she would make a great nurse. She knew she could succeed and although she cried some, panicked often before tests and even thought about believing all those who told her to find another goal, she was determined they would not be right. What gave her that level of com-mitment, that drive, that faith in her dream? I believe it was Stacey's belief in herself and her faith in God! The irony is that as a little girl she was easily discouraged by losses and negative comments. She was beautiful and kind, yet she was easily hurt by the thoughtless taunts of classmates. She struggled with attention deficit disorder and the disap-pointment of being raised in a single parent home. Somewhere in that young heart and with a lot of lecturing from her mom about "nobody can keep you from doing what you want to do," this young woman found herself. Stacey discovered the perseverance that led her to change schools, take extra courses and work even more intensely toward her goal. She graduated from Nursing School. It took seven years, almost as long as becoming a lawyer or a doctor, but she did it! She gained so much more than a nursing degree. Stacey has found affirmation of who she is and strength from her belief in herself!

Who are you? Have you ever asked yourself that question? It has been said in the book of Isaiah, "You have no right to argue with your Creator. You are a clay pot shaped by your potter. Does the clay ask, 'Why did you make me this way?'"

Use one of the blank pages in the back of the book to write down who you are. If you are stumped as to how to describe yourself, pretend you are your mom and write what you think she would answer. Then, be another family member, a friend, a co-worker, anyone who spends time with you.

Look at yourself in different roles of your life. When you are at work, what is different about you than when you are at home or at play? How do you react in the midst of a stressful situation or a crisis?

THE QUIZ

The father asked his daughter, "Are you an egg, a carrot, or a coffee bean?" She looked at him with a puzzled expression. "I don't know what you mean, daddy." He suggested she come into the kitchen with him, and he proceeded to pull out three seemingly unrelated objects...an egg, a carrot and a coffee bean. "Which one are you? Think about this egg. It is so fragile. If it slipped out of my hand, it would shatter all over the floor. Now this carrot is just the opposite. I could throw it against the wall, and it wouldn't be hurt. Then, there's this coffee bean. It is hard and really not very tasty when you bite into it." At this point, his daughter was becoming irritated. "Dad, I gotta go." Pulling out a pot, filling it with water and placing it on the stove, the Dad asked his daughter, "What happens to these things when they are thrown into hot water?" She stared at the stove. Quietly, she said, "I think I know what you are trying to tell me. The egg gets hard and strong. It won't break. The carrot gets mushy and weak. But, I don't know what the coffee bean means."

"It becomes flavorful and tasty bringing a change to those who drink it. Which are you, honey?" he asked her.

Which are you? Think about your reaction to stressful situations and crises. "A crisis event often explodes the illusions that anchor our lives," according to Robert Veninga, author of *A Gift of Hope*. It is extremely important that you know who you are when the unexpected throws you off track. Where do you turn for direction? Can you stay true to the course if you don't know what resources to call upon from deep inside your psyche? I say be proactive and have a clear understanding of your strengths and weaknesses long before you must make changes or deal with attacks on your self image that threaten your belief in yourself. We show our truest self when we are hurt or in pain. We find our focus when we are challenged or our peace of mind is threatened.

Look again at the description of yourself...

Do you believe in this person?

Do you trust yourself?

Can you be strong enough to weather the challenges of life?

Does the value of your name mean anything to you?

Is loyalty and trust an important part of who you are?

Are you the final stop in making a choice for yourself?

Think about these things!

As you evaluate yourself, you will realize that the purpose you have chosen or that has been chosen for you by a loving God must be basis for the tracks upon which your life's train runs. If the world throws the switch to send you off on a side rail, you must be ready to switch back to the main track at the first opportunity. For some people, life is easier. Their train never seems to move from the path it was set on. But for the rest of us, we are constantly fighting the threat of our own distractions and vices. I am sure you have

> *"Experience is not what happens to you. It is what you do with what happens to you."*
>
> Aldous Huxley
> Author

read a multitude of quotes even entire books about how to stay focused. My suggestion is simple and somewhat elementary...I shared it with you in Chapter Three.

Find five minutes for reflection before your day begins. You may read it, pray it, think it, speak it. Then, looking in the mirror, BE SURE to compliment yourself and ask yourself if your life is still on the main track you dreamed it would be. SMILE! ENJOY! SUCCEED!

In the first half of the twentieth century, humility was the asset all wanted to possess. "Never seek recognition or brag about your successes. People will think you are conceited, and you will never be liked." In the sixties, seventies, and eighties, the pendulum gradually swung far to the other side. "If I don't shout my praises and draw attention to my abilities and attributes, no one else will." The phrase, "It's all about me!" began to emerge and indeed, was the catch phrase of the nineties. Yet, there did not seem to be the joy in self-centeredness that many had thought.

Joy versus happiness... joy is a deep feeling of contentment... happiness is learning to enjoy living in the moment.

Are you joyful or happy?

The twenty first century is evolving as a time of reality and sensibility. Has the pendulum stopped in the center? Being confident is considered strengthening and appropriate. Realizing that we have responsibilities and that we are given gifts to be discovered, cultivated and contributed is important. Sharing our faith is not only acceptable, but crosses all media from politics to television. Taking care of ourselves demands we be proud and believe it is acceptable to seek our "best self."

And one more thing...be your own cheerleader! Whoever invented the concept that you shouldn't be proud of your accomplishments or reward yourself for a job well done is probably a person who doesn't know or believe in himself. One idea to ensure you keep yourself enthusiastic about YOU is to start an "I Like Me" file. It is actually very simple. Gather any and everything positive that has ever been written or given to you that builds your ego or compliments you for a job well done. Put it in this file and pull it out whenever you doubt yourself or feel like you have lost your focus. The world may forget to compliment you...the boss may not recognize the contributions you make...your loved ones may take you for granted, but you must remember how amazing you are. Let this file be a gift to yourself in those moments of doubt!

"Be gentle with yourself. If you will not be your own unconditional friend, who will be? If you are playing an opponent and you are also opposing your-self... you are going to be outnumbered."

Dan Millman
Way of the Peaceful Mind

Author, Catherine Aird once said, "If you can't be a good example, then you'll just have to be a horrible warning." May we all go through life sharing the best that we are and always believing that our place on this earth is meaningful!

Before leaving this chapter, think again about who you are…

Write a press release about your life. Fill it with the things of which you are proud, the skills you possess, the friends you value. In this release share your faith and from whence it comes. Then, seal it and mail it to yourself.

Will you be amazed and proud of the person you portray?

The fourth chapter of the *Magnificent Seven Plus ONE* is a key to your success. Know yourself, and then believe!

CHAPTER FIVE

No Matter What Your Age, Always Be a Dreamer

"We grow great by dreams...Some of us let our dreams die, but others nourish and protect them, nurse them through bad days 'til they bring them to sunshine and light."

Woodrow Wilson
President of the United States

God does not give us a dream without the means to fulfill it! That's what I always told my daughters.

In 1923, Mary Breckinridge rode her horse into the impoverished "hollers" of Kentucky's Appalachian Mountains. She was raised in affluence all over the world and was a descendent of the blue-blood Kentucky Breckinridge family. She was a nurse and had been instrumental in the recovery efforts in France after World War I.

Mary Breckinridge had been divorced and widowed. She had lost a daughter at infancy and a son at four. She dreamed of helping the people she saw in the tiny mountain cabins and was determined to lower the staggeringly high infant mortality rate in those hills of Kentucky. She traveled to Scotland where she trained to be a nurse mid-wife and there envisioned the impact she could make in Kentucky with the skills she gained. Remember, she DREAMED of helping these people!

When Miss Breckinridge determined to provide better obstetrical service here, she was faced with the fact that midwifery has only partial recognition in the United States…For this reason, it was necessary to import midwives trained in Europe or to send American nurses abroad for training…At first, the mountain people were very suspicious of the "brought on women" and continued to have their babies "cotched by the grannies."

Woman's Journal
"The Nurse on Horseback"

She made her dream her life's work when in 1925, at the age of forty-four she opened the Frontier Nursing Service. This amazing organization has literally given birth to thousands of children who otherwise may never have survived. It has trained hundreds of nurses to go where physicians do not. It has provided healthcare first at very rudimentary outposts, and today at a hospital named after Ms. Breckinridge. There are now degrees in mid-wifery at the universities surrounding the Appalachian's that have been preparing the Frontier Nurses of the future to go all over the world where they may serve those unable to serve themselves. There is even a most meaningful courier program which allows college age women to live at FNS outposts and act as aides to the nurses and staff.

> *"If one advances*
> *confidently in the*
> *direction of his dreams*
> *and endeavors to live*
> *the life which he has*
> *imagined, he will meet*
> *with a success unexpected*
> *in common hours."*
>
> *Henry David Thoreau*
> *Poet*

Look at what one dream has done for so many. It was only a dream, but it became Mary Breckinridge's life work! She once said, "I have not gone in there to help a blooming soul. I have gone in, in response to an obvious need realized by the people themselves who are anxious to cooperate. They are fine, intelligent citizens." What is your dream?

At seventy-eight, she faces the palette, watercolors by her side. The glorious San Gabrielle mountains loom before her as the sun begins to ease its glistening rays into the dissolving darkness. She smiles because she knows this will be a morning filled with the hues of color she loves to imitate in her paintings. She has sold only a few since she first picked up the brush in her early twenties. But, that really does not matter to her. Her dream is to paint not to see her work hanging in the Louvre.

Abraham's wife Sara was too old to bear a child. Yet, she dreamed it and prayed to God for His gift. In Genesis, God would give her even more than she had dreamed of. "Then, God said to Abraham…I will bless Sara, and indeed I will give you a son by her. She shall be a mother of nations. Kings of peoples will come from her."

Since childhood, the fifty year-old man had always loved horses. He wanted to own one, but lived in the city and traveled too much. Yet, he found himself captivated each time he passed a meadow with the grandeur of a mare at full gallop, her foal just behind. He was sure this dream of owning a horse would elude him. Not so. Creatively, he devised a way to fulfill his dream. It is called co-leasing. He would have half interest in a horse splitting the boarding fee and riding anytime he wanted considering it did not exceed the other owner's rights. He's ecstatic that a childhood dream has become a reality in his mid-life years.

Think your dream is unachievable? Embarrassed because friends and family do not really understand? Ignore the naysayers! When someone comments judgmentally that they have no idea what you think you are doing, just invite them along for the "ride." Let them experience something new and then, see how they react.

It is amazing to note that in this day of corporate scandals and cries for legalizing gay marriages, there have been a multitude of television news programs, as well as national, well-respected magazines and newspapers talking about religion and a unique life, that of Jesus Christ. This has all been prompted by one man's "Passion." At the risk of destroying a fabulously successful acting career, Mel Gibson openly and very publicly, shared his faith with the world. It was his dream to bring reality to the Biblical stories of the crucifixion of Christ.

"I had to do it!" he said repeatedly when interviewed about his reason for risking his own money and his entire life's work. "This is what God wanted me to do."

Often our dreams are just that...the picture of where God wants us to be! We will explore this further in Chapter 8. Is there something gnawing away at you and constantly popping up in your dreams that may be trying to guide your waking moments?

Dreaming is deeply ingrained in all of us from the moment we are born. Have you ever watched a tiny baby sleeping and suddenly her little mouth erupts into a giant grin? What joyous dream could one so young be having?

Try this exercise to capture the dreams of your life...

When you were ten years old and younger, what things did you enjoy doing? List them all and the ages you remember doing them. What rewards spurred you on?

When you were between the ages of eleven and sixteen, what did you enjoy? Be specific and tell how well you excelled. Be honest, too. What incentives/ guidance moved you forward?

From seventeen to twenty-five, what was/is fun for you? Do you need rewards, incentives, prizes, accolades to be happy?

What do you do today for enjoyment? Relate it to your youth. Are there any carry-overs or similarities? Why or why not? Is your work also your enjoyment?

You have 48 hours to do WHATEVER will make you happy. Be realistic, BUT don't let finances or schedules deter your wishes. Be honest about who you want with you, if anyone. Describe how you will spend that time, then start making plans to do it! Put a date on paper to fulfill your dream.

JESSICA'S STORY

Jessica Grové is a beautiful and talented young woman from Columbus, Ohio. Her dream was to be "On Broadway." Her parents embraced that dream with loving support and valuable training. "We have never pushed Jessica in this direction; she has always motivated herself. Our only role has been to be the facilitators to make this possible. That, for us, is the fulfillment of our dream."

The dreams guiding my life are first and foremost dreams of continued love and happiness. I do aspire to become a better performer and to be in the spotlight, but no amount of acceptance from an audience is as real or fulfilling as being happy with myself and loving the person I am.

I started thinking about this in the past year or so. I have achieved many of my dreams but put a part of myself on hold. I have dreams of becoming a great Broadway star or film actor, but there is a harsh reality. There is a lot of competition out there. I am on Broadway, I have a decent following, but as great as all that is, a part of me didn't feel complete. This is when I realized that dreams could be more than being famous. I dream of knowing myself and finding happiness in life.

My family, specifically my mom and dad, endorsed my dream of being a Broadway performer. They supported me and sacrificed years of their own lives because they saw in me a talent and a passion for performing. I have a huge support system, from my parents, my brother, grandparents, aunts, uncles, cousins and friends to a boyfriend who supports anything I want or need to do. I am so fortunate to have the love and support that everyone in this world should have, but may not be lucky enough to have, which is why my newest quest is to take that love and apply it towards bettering myself and being there for those I love.

I had a natural singing ability and a big imagination from the time I was a little girl. I once convinced my friends that the window in my family's kitchen was a drive through bakery! At ten years old I began taking voice lessons to learn how to use my instrument. My voice teacher Marjorie Stephens was a constant source of support. I took part in community theatre productions around town, which taught me focus and gave me experience.

I am currently in the ensemble of a Broadway show. I am so thankful to have a job. I am living my initial dream to a certain extent.

Broadway is where I had hoped to be and I've made it! It's all a bit sur-real. In the next year I would love to get another show and take on a new challenge. In the next five years I hope to still be in the business. I may even go to college to study to become a teacher. I would love to teach and inspire very young children. I know that it is something that would bring a smile to my face daily.

Although my dreams have morphed a bit, I continue to dare to dream. If one doesn't have a dream or two, then what is there to look forward to? Most of the time great things don't come to those who sit idly.

As of April, 2004, Jessica is in another Broadway Show!

THAT JIMINY CRICKETT...

What a smart guy he was. Now, he didn't say that if you were under ten or under twenty or under thirty, anything your heart desires will come to you. He just said you should wish. He forgot to mention that often times a lot of hard work, commitment and planning goes into some of these dream fulfillments, but that's okay 'cause the point is you should never stop dreaming and for sure, never stop believing those dreams will come true.

And, thus, the impetus for my own crazy dream. At the age of fifty, I decided I wanted to compete in a beauty pageant...complete with interview, evening gown and, yes, the infamous bathing suit competition. Now, what makes this all the more interesting is that the pageant I chose had two criteria for participating. One was you had to be married...it was the Mrs. Ohio United States Pageant... and the other was you had to be over 18. Think about that. I am fifty and could potentially walk the runway against an 18 year old in a bathing suit. I began to doubt my own belief that what I lacked in youthful skin I made up for in life experiences.

BUT, I did not waiver in my dream. I set forward on a plan that has been my lifestyle for the past four years. First of all, I found a great trainer who decided to change the way I ate. I have always been a blatant sweets freak. I love my sugar and my chocolate. I have worn this proudly for years on my hips, my waist and a few other very visible places. But, those extra bulges would never do in a bathing suit under spotlights. So, I went for the protein diet. Not really the Atkins or the South Beach Diet, just my own brand of focusing on lean meats, eggs for breakfast with that Turkey bacon, fish any way except fried or breaded and of course, salads. (I get all my dressings and sauces on the side if I am eating out, and I never use butter.) Notice, no mention of fruits, bread or pasta. That is because I never have it. In fact, my rule is "Nothing white!" That means no potatoes, sugar, flour, pasta, white bread...wheat is great, only I always get the thin sliced...you get the picture.

Now, don't get me wrong I am not perfect. In fact, I have to admit that after the first few weeks of this, I was craving anything I couldn't have, especially my chocolate. So, my trainer said, "Once a week, take a binge day and have whatever you want. Think of it as a reward for your efforts. Then, get right back on the routine." By the way, it is not a diet. You get off of those. This is an eating routine that has worked for me. What are the results? I dropped two dress sizes in eight weeks and except for a couple of pounds, I am still that size four.

Did I mention I had a trainer? A great young man...Mike, who should be called "Attila the Hun" for the torturous workout regimen he started me on. I kept telling him to remember I was over fifty and couldn't do what his young athletes could. He ignored me and pressed on. He knew I had discovered YOGA the year I turned fifty, and he knew I was an avid golfer with a handicap in the teens and that I had my sites set on becoming a good tennis player. But, all he wanted to do was turn me into a "lean, mean pageant winning machine!" So, we worked hard those first six months. I walked, not ran, because I was worried about the knees...or I did 2 to 3 miles either on the treadmill or outside six days a week. I did, and still do, a pace of about four miles an hour. We lifted weights to get the flab under the arms. We did squats and lunges and Mike's favorite, straddle jumps with a bar that I hold in both my hands horizontally and thrust toward the ceiling. Three reps of everything. Then, there were the memorable "ab" routines which included crunches, feet up in the air and twist to touch opposite toes, pelvic tilts and my favorite, standing facing a clock and sucking my stomach in for one minute. Yes, three reps of all this, too. You CAN try all this at home or in your local gym, just be careful when lifting weights not to get them too heavy. A good rule of thumb is if you can do 10 to 15, you have the right weight. Ask the trainer in the gym to advise you. Maybe you can find your own Attila the Hun to help motivate you.

I found time to continue my YOGA, because it compliments working out. You stretch muscles and improve balance, but most importantly, YOGA helps you clear your mind and focus on yourself and your body. It is wonderful for any body type and any age.

The results of all this excruciating physical work were almost immediate. I could not believe it. I have watched my weight and exercised my whole life, but I have never seen such dramatic results so quickly. I did not check my weight often. Weighing in once a week at the same time in the morning is so much better than everyday, because honestly, as for the ladies, our weight fluctuates just like our moods once we hit menopause. Right? Instead of reading the scales, I just let the way my clothes fit show me the rewards of my efforts.

It was so much fun to see results. And, now working out is a routine for me. If I am traveling, I find a treadmill and walk on. When I am mentally fatigued, I do a few YOGA moves. I would be lying if I said I couldn't wait for every day when I worked out with Mike, but he just laughed and remained patient with me. And, remember, once a week I have my "splurge day" when I have my Graeter's ice cream and my pasta. So, I still do allow myself a break!

There is one more vitally important thing that I did to prepare myself for this unique sport of pageantry. I focused on my mental and spiritual self. I found ten to fifteen minutes a day, usually in the morning to read the Bible or a motivational book. I would often sit just looking out the window for some inspirational moment. A rainbow, a tiny ant lifting a twig, a mother bird feeding her babies, my cat jumping at some invisible intruder. These quiet moments are our renewing exercises and for me a reminder that there is a higher power in charge. This quiet time also allows me to focus on the volunteer work that I love to do and the impact I want to make on my platform issues of mental health and children in need.

So, now you have my story. I looked at my fiftieth birthday and thought, "I can hate it. I can go crazy and get a red sports car with a twenty-year-old boyfriend. I can climb into my room and eat myself silly, or I can get excited about the next half of my life's century and do pageants." When my astonished husband and my three grown daughters...yes, they are the same age as the ladies I compete against...tried to dissuade me, I just told them that there was a lot worse trouble I could get into after fifty than being in a beauty contest and dreaming of winning.

And how have I done? I was first runner-up in my very first pageant, the Mrs. Ohio United States, to a twenty-five year old. The next year, I was first runner-up again. I lost by only two-tenths of a point in that pageant and won second runner-up in the Mrs. Ohio America. I continued being in the top three in both of these pageants until I won a new pageant in 2003 called "Ms. Ohio Senior". This competition was for any woman married, single, widowed or divorced who is over fifty. Then, in Tampa, Florida, I was crowned Mrs. All American 2003, a national pageant for ladies over 35 and married five years or more.

It has been an exciting and rewarding journey. What do you want to do? What is your dream? Go for it. You will feel so young and revitalized. I am no different than you! I am just a real believer that no one is ever too old to try something new, especially if they pray about it and work hard to achieve it. Remember the end of Jiminy's song? "No request is too extreme. When you wish upon a star your dreams come true!"

While in New York in January, 2002, I met Kimberly Hamill Dresch, an artist who is also an NBC News Audio person. This woman embodies the people of her beloved city. As the quintessential New Yorker, she believes that for the fast-paced citizens, self-actualization is key. Soon after I met her, Kimberly would survive uterine cancer at the age of 46. Kimberly says...

Dreams are self-realization, so it's probably important to understand where you are in your life at all times...that takes prescient living, something that can't be taught, but perhaps inspired. What one dreams about is only one aspect of how we become who we are in our families, professions and community. My dream is to stay healthy in order to see grandchildren and to enjoy a wonderful creatively active retirement... where I'll become a productive member of that community.

It is an amazing moment when we finally realize so much of our heart and mind is released in the quiet of our dreams. In the Bible, Joseph was spared from the slavery his brothers tricked him into by his ability to interpret the king's dreams. Like so many of his time, Joseph knew that what the mind conjured in its sleep posed a message for the waking moments. What have you dreamed of lately? Is it the result of what you had for your evening meal or the outcome of a stressful day? According to Kimberly Dresch, "Our dreams have spiritual implications for they steer us toward our potential as human beings..." Do our dreams reveal a deeply held desire that won't be suppressed...completely? The next time you awaken from a dream, write it down as descriptively as possible. Are your heart and mind trying to tell you something?

A young man from a tiny golf course in Central Ohio called Mill Run won the 2003 British Open. Who would have guessed it? Who dreamed it? Ben Curtis did and his dream became a reality.

Barry Manilow has a song entitled *I Made it Through the Rain* that embodies the reason having dreams is so essential to our lives.

I Made it Through the Rain

We dreamers have our ways of facing rainy days

And somehow we survive…

We keep the feelings warm,

Protect them from the storm, until our time arrives….

Then, one day the sun appears..

And, we come shining through those lonely years!

I made it through the rain…I kept my world protected

I made it through the rain…I kept my point of view.

I made it through the rain and found myself respected by the others who…

Got rained on, too, and made it through!!!

When friends are hard to find and life seems so unkind,

Sometimes you feel afraid!

Just think beyond the clouds and rise above the crowds

And start your own parade!

'Cause when I chase my fears away, that's when

I knew that I could finally say,

I made it through the rain. I kept my world protected

I made it through the rain, I kept my point of view

I made it through the rain and found myself

respected…by the others who…

Got rained on, too, and made it through!!!

I made it through the rain. I kept my world protected.

I made it through the rain. I kept my point of view

I made it through the rain and found myself respected by the others who.

Got rained on, too, and made it through.

And made it through…

And Made It Through!!!

Now look deeply into your own mind…

What do you dream of when you dream?

How do our dreams become our goals?

How do you convince yourself and others that these dreams are realistic?

Where do you find the resources to fulfill the dreams you dream?

I contend that it comes from somewhere deep inside…that small voice continuously urging us forward into the unknown. That same voice challenges us to learn more and live more and believe more!

Why would someone over fifty dream of winning a beauty contest? As I said in my application…

> Being crowned Mrs. All American would epitomize my landing a fabulous, full-time job! The honor would mean the judges have seen in me the best of today's mature, married woman who is grounded by her values, her commitment to her family and her faith.

For me, this dream was motivation. It was a way to encapsulate all the experiences of my life into an opportunity to share…maybe even inspire someone I might never know otherwise.

No matter what you dream, remember that it is empowering to see success and excitement at the end of that proverbial tunnel. We all need a dream. It keeps us invigorated. It keeps us young. It keeps us looking around each corner for a new opportunity, a new experience. Remember that dreams can be a pathway for God's guidance. We may not always fulfill our dreams, but how powerful the journey can be. We need to have visions of change while still appreciating the joys around us. Is it a dream to share laughter with a little child? It is if the child is your own or your grandchild. Is it a dream to read words that make our lives blessed and fulfilled? It is if your heart has longed for the message you see. If we can dream it, we can achieve it!

CHAPTER SIX

Surround Yourself With People Who Understand, Care and Support

"The ability to cultivate relationships is the most important skill in life for it affects every decision and supports all efforts at success."

Kimberly Hamill Dresch
Artist, NBC Network News Technician

The pronouncement from the doctor could not have been worse. "It is cancer." Karen listened, but wonders still today if she really heard. She had been diagnosed with Stage IV breast cancer. Her life would never be the same. Then, she thought of them...the four women who had been with her nearly her entire life. She knew their love would embrace her at this challenging time. She was blessed, she would proclaim, to be understood and unfailingly cared for. Karen knew they would help her get through this nightmare. And, she was right! "All of the women in my support group have been friends for a lifetime. Betsy, Sharon and I first became friends in 1957 when 'our gang' began in fourth grade. My friend Diane and I met right after college in 1969 when she came from Chicago. Pam and I have been friends since birth. I am the common thread in the friendship of the five of us."

Karen knew that her best medicine would be to surround herself with these women. Sharon and Betsy sprang into action. There was daily communication via e-mail, because Sharon was in St. Thomas while Betsy was in Florida. Each day, the three women would read the same passage from *Journey to the Heart* by Melodie Beattie, and Karen would read a daily quote from *Conversations with God* by Neale Donald Walsh that Sharon had sent. Both women traveled to Columbus for the "worst summer of my life" as Karen underwent chemotherapy.

After the sobering news, Karen received a visit from Diane. She paraded into her friend's home dressed in a red formal ball gown and tiara. Karen's laughter was stronger medicine than any of the chemo and radiation the doctors could ever prescribe. Diane was like that...the strong, direct, funny friend who had once needed the other four to support her through the end of a marriage and the disdainful conversations surrounding it. She owed it to Karen to lighten the load of this nearly unbearable news. Diane believes you have to get past the bad things to know yourself. Pam is beside Karen, constantly offering the solace of her seaside home in Florida and laughter over adventures they have shared.

> *"Separate reeds are weak and easily broken, but bound together, they are strong and hard to tear apart."*
>
> The Midrash
> Jewish Scripture

These women embodied the truth that you can give without loving, but you cannot love without giving!

Karen is today strong and inspiring. Her four friends continue enveloping her with their love and encouragement.

During a second grade exercise, students were asked to define love. One little girl said, "When my grandmother got arthritis, she couldn't bend over to paint her toenails anymore. So, my grandfather does it for her all the time even when his hands got arthritis, too. That's love." Out of the mouths of babes.

My two precious step-granddaughters ages four and three, unpretentiously grab "Grandma Donna's" hand and demand I watch *The Lion King* or play *Candyland*. The glow in their eyes and their contagious giggles remind me that there is strength in the simplest things. Being surrounded by these bubbly little girls keeps me from becoming totally engulfed in the diversions of adulthood. They don't realize how important they are to my support system, but they will someday.

Author and lecturer Leo Buscalia once talked about a contest he was asked to judge. The purpose of the contest was to find the most caring child. The winner was a four year old whose next door neighbor was an elderly gentleman who had recently lost his wife. Upon seeing the man cry, the little boy went into the old gentleman's yard, climbed onto his lap and just sat there. When his mother asked him what he had said to the neighbor, the little boy said, "Nothing. I just helped him cry." Clearly, it is not with words, but by offering time and concern, by caring, that we show our support.

Deep in the heart of Kentucky, there exists a town called Hodgenville. As the birthplace of Abraham Lincoln, you would think this place would be known all over the country, but alas, everyone thinks he was born in Illinois. So, this wonderful little town longs for recognition and respect. Yet, it is in the love of its citizens that recognition thrives. There, people share the joys and pain of each other's lives. There, lifelong friendships are nurtured. Students grow up to socialize with their teachers. Sons work with fathers. Mothers care for their daughters' daughters. Love is the thread that ties the town together. And even when you leave, the bond is not broken, only stretched like a giant rubber band that magically pulls you back into its embrace when you need nurturing.

I moved there as a newlywed, taught school and developed friendships that have weathered over thirty years…new babies, marriages, job changes, moves and divorces. I learned prioritization of family and work. I discovered my love of speaking, writing and working with the media. I became an entrepreneur launching a small business that empowered me to find the humility to let God lead me to my next destination.

Without the blanket of love that enveloped me for eleven years, I may not have found the strength to grow. The friends of 1975 are still my friends today. They allowed me to stumble and applauded me when I succeeded. They supported me when my decisions seemed questionable. They saluted me when I headed off to another adventure. But most importantly, they understand my faith drives my inner passions, and they want me to fulfill them.

> *"I find the great thing in life is not where we stand so much as where we are moving."*
> *Oliver Wendell Holmes*
> *Author, Physician*

Did you come from a place like Hodgenville?

How have your roots affected your life?

Do you have a circle of friends who know how far you have come and what growth you have undergone? Who are they? Do they know how dear they are to you?

Now would be the ideal time to call or write. Tell them how immeasurably important they have been to you. And, if possible, touch their hand or enthusiastically hug them the next time you are together. For like our friend Karen, everyone finds strength from knowing they are loved and feeling the touch of an unwavering friendship.

Did you know the sense of touch is the first to develop and the last to fail? Do you feel uncomfortable when someone you care about touches you? If the answer is yes, ask yourself why. Is it because we question the sincerity? Do you feel unworthy? Think of how often the Bible talks about touching those we care about. It is one of our best unspoken gestures of concern and love.

BUSINESS RELATIONSHIPS

When you are in the workplace or even a volunteer situation, do you believe those around you care how you feel and support your goals? If they disagree with you, will you value those thoughts? Or do you ignore, maybe even eliminate them from your circle of advisors?

In his book, *On Leadership*, John Gardner contends that the best leader is one who ensures that the appropriate talent and skill are built into the team. "If the leader is a visionary," Gardner says, "he needs to have people around him who are practical and are gifted in setting an agenda." I would add to this if you have to choose between a brilliant mind with no common sense and an average intelligence with tremendous common sense, go for the latter.

Now, whether you are a leader or a follower, it is forever true that surrounding yourself with people who know you well and who care about you is the key to success. Note, I did not say they have to think like you do or enjoy what you enjoy or even like the same sports that you do. They just have to care sincerely and understand what you wish to accomplish in life. Surrounding yourself with people who understand you ensures a lifeline in times of crisis, but more importantly, a sounding board for your ideas and emotions.

Ask yourself...

Surround Yourself With People Who Understand, Care and Support

Who do you go to when you have a new idea or a concern?

Does this person really care what you are saying and doing?

What makes this person essential in your life?

Can you be honest with them?

When George W. Bush ran for President of the United States in 1999, one of the most damaging criticisms was his lack of experience in foreign affairs. Take a moment to think about that and where this President was in the spring of 2004. Why is he so confident in his ability to

> *"People are lonely because they build walls not bridges".*
> Joseph Fort Newton
> Minister

manage the impending problems and the crushing crises in places all around the globe? Because he wisely surrounded himself with brilliant people who know foreign affairs. They are loyal as well as knowledgeable. They understand this President's agenda and care deeply about him as a person. Dick Cheney, Vice President; Colin Powell, Secretary of State; Donald Rumsfeld, Secretary of Defense; Condoleeza Rice, National Security Advisor all leaders in their own right, but friends who chose to be a part of a committed team. They embody the sixth of the *Magnificent Seven Plus ONE*...surround yourself with people who understand, care and support.

The CEO of Columbus, Ohio based Eastway Supplies Inc. meets monthly with all of his employees in four separate team meetings to evaluate the progress of the company's success. Surrounding themselves with a culture of understanding and caring, the associates focus on Tim Kight's business concept called Architects of Change. These five imperatives form the foundation of the company's goals...

1. *Build a Strong Foundation*
2. *Pay Exceptional Attention to the Marketplace*
3. *Focus On Core Processes*
4. *Organize for Performance*
5. *Create a Personal Best Culture*

Another successful U.S. company believes it must be a strong, close-knit group to ensure success. The founders exemplify the positives of surrounding yourself with people who know and care. Helene and Marvin Gralnick started Chico's in 1983 as a folk art company selling Mexican and South American items on Sanibel Island. Helene began designing clothes and the story goes that Marvin made the first mannequins by having Helene lay on a board so he could trace around her silhouette. To this day, the Chico's clothes are displayed on duplicates of his wife. Their business has become one of the most successful in the highly competitive women's clothing market, yet they insist on surrounding themselves exclusively with associates who understand and support their goals.

In their welcome to new associates, the Garlnick's proclaim, "Every team member is unique. We value your individuality, and we look forward to your efforts contributing to our success."

CHICO's 1983 – 2003 Teamwork

1. *Respect for All*	10. *Honesty*
2. *Communication*	11. *Overcoming Obstacles*
3. *Achieving Goals*	12. *Innovative Energy*
4. *Trust*	13. *Fun*
5. *Recognition*	14. *Confidence*
6. *Developing Others*	15. *Personal Growth*
7. *Fairness*	16. *Random Acts of Kindness*
8. *Individual Commitment*	17. *Entrepreneurial Spirit*
9. *Positive Attitude*	18. *Creativity*

The Old Testament, Numbers 14:24, tells us of Caleb who thought differently than his boss, but still "followed his master completely!"

Wouldn't it be ideal if each employee were as supportive as Caleb of his leader, but more importantly, cared enough about the direction his leader was going to support the decisions made?

"Beware of who you are and admit your faults," said Arnold Schwarzenegger during a February, 2004 *Meet the Press* television appearance when asked what he thinks makes for a good leader. And, I would add, then find the people skilled where you are lacking!

The phenomenon of Donald Trump's reality television show *The Apprentice* emphasized the truth that you win with caring, understanding and supportive team members. The chosen apprentice, Bill, wisely surrounded himself with the brightest and the best of his former competitors when managing his final test. His team wanted him to succeed. They understood what tasks were needed to provide the best outcome. They cared if he was the winner and thus, supported his decisions while sharing their creativity and talents in a way that Bill would be successful. Overall, each person worked unselfishly to reach their goal...seeing Bill become *The Apprentice*. The loser, Kwame, chose team members with agendas unrelated to his success. His people did not share his vision nor did they seem to care if he won. It appeared that several of the three team members wanted only to be in charge themselves. A real recipe for disaster.

Who is on your team?

Why are they beside you?

Have you ever told them how valuable they are to you? Explain.

A REAL BUDDY

The farmer sitting on his tractor saw the young man running up to him totally out of breath. He said he had gotten his SUV stuck in the muddy area way back in the woods and could the farmer please help. "I can't get my tractor back there 'cause of the thick trees."

"How'd you get back there anyway?" said the farmer, "Doesn't matter no way. I can get my 'Buddy' back there." The young man looked a bit confused until the farmer added, "He's my horse."

The farmer turned and sauntered slowly to the stall. Out came a huge black draft horse with a twinkle in his eye, and the farmer patiently harnessed him up to two huge lines with big grappling hooks on the end. "We pull big logs up with these. I reckon I can get your truck out of trouble."

He tightened the leather lines around his big workhorse and adjusted the bit for maximum contact with "his friend." The farmer clicked to the horse and said, "Giddy up, old Nellie." Well, the horse didn't move. The farmer clicked again, this time, "Move on out, Blackie" no movement out of the horse. The young man was getting really agitated but held his tongue. Again, the farmer clicked, "Let's move it, Ray." Not a quiver from the big old black horse. "Alright, Buddy," he yelled. As he popped the lines, he said, "Let's get moving." With one huge lunge, the giant draft horse jerked the truck right out of the mire, pulled it away from further entrapment and paused with the tightening of the farmer's rein.

The young man was amazed. "Why did you call him all those names and why didn't he move the first three times?"

"Well," the old farmer said, "You see it's real simple. Buddy doesn't think he can do anything by himself, so I just make him think there are other horses helping him, and he moves right on out!" The farmer knew Buddy and how to bring out his best. Buddy believed he had friends to help. Little did he know that the best friend was the one holding the reins.

Surround Yourself With People Who Understand, Care and Support

Who is holding your reins? Sound strange, but that is figuratively what happens in relationships. Someone has a hold of you to either guide you or support you or push you or hug you or to hold you back. What is it you need right now? To feel understood and cared for? How valuable are the characteristics of loyalty, trust, honesty and conscience? Can you pick up the phone and share your feelings? Life cannot truly be lived and fulfilled without those opportunities to share and grow and feel loved. We were not made to wander through life alone, and life's support may come from the most unlikely of sources.

Consider the story of the successful single businesswoman. She owned her own home, her own car, attended all the right functions and was accepted into the highest levels of government. Yet, she turned to a foster child for strength. Her initial reason was philanthropic…to be a Big Sister to this eight-year-old girl, but the relationship quickly became reciprocal. The times of playing and movies and talking and making cookies became real food for this woman's soul. In hoping to surround a child with love and understanding, she had found someone who gave these wonderful qualities right back to her.

Have you ever found yourself in a situation like this? Your plan was to be a help to someone else, but you quickly find the roles have reversed. You have a new source of support and caring.

IN HALLIE'S EYES

As I lifted the veil, I saw in my daughter's eyes the reflection of the future and peace with the past. I had always dreamed of Hallie's wedding day praying that she would find a great love and bring to her new life the same strength, grace and joy that she had always given me. She stood before me, a beautiful woman full of excitement and contentment. The years of dance classes and lacrosse games, proms and diving meets, schoolbooks and church trips flashed before me in the quiet of that moment.

She was my savior. I would never have survived the divorce and the eight years of single mothering without Hallie. As we moved from the only home she had ever known, this seven year old stared up at me and said, "Don't cry, Mommy. I love you!" In her eyes, I was the strong and wise one who would navigate these strange new waters and keep her safe. Little did she know that it was my fierce desire to shield her from sadness and provide for her that kept me going. She gave me peace in the midst of turmoil. She never judged or questioned. Hallie only trusted that whatever I did was the best for her and her little sisters.

Through the laughter and the tears, her eyes forever revealed her faith that we would weather life's challenges together. Those precious eyes still affirm that angels do live on earth and that miracles come in the form of little girls with blonde curls. I looked at my dear Hallie as I released the veil and saw in her eyes the wonderful, caring woman every mother prays to call her daughter! And, I thanked God for this priceless gift!

> *"All the beautiful sentiments in the world weigh less than a single lovely action."*
> *James Russell*
> *Orator, Poet*

People often appear in our lives without warning…people who change us forever. They come as total strangers to give us answers to a pressing problem. Has that ever happened to you? Where do they come from?

In his small, but amazingly successful book *The Prayer of Jabez*, Bruce Wilkinson talks about "Jabez moments." These are times when we inexplicably meet a new person and what they share with us (or we with them) brings enlightenment or relief. How could they know to ask the questions they ask or make the comments they do? It was just the thing we needed to hear. Wilkinson believes it is God surrounding us with people who know and care when we need them the most.

Ask yourself…

When was the last time someone was there when you needed them the most?

How could they know to say those things?

How could they be so reassuring, so comforting?

I believe God sent them to you!

As challenging teenagers, two girls were experimenting with drinking and marijuana. They wanted to fit in. They needed to feel special. They were looking in every direction for confirmation of their worth. And, then, they heard about "Young Life." This non-denominational, Christian group focuses on what is happening to high school students and what their positive responses should be. The girls joined their friends in large meetings at first where they laughed at the volunteer college students as they spoofed popular music and challenging situations that the kids might have encountered. "Young Life" had smaller groups that offered more intimate discussions. The two girls were able to share their fears and their apprehensions with both leaders and peers. Each gathering ended with discussions of "What Would Jesus Do?" and prayer.

Through "Young Life," these blossoming young women found meaning and focus. They matured while learning how to face whatever the world might throw at them. The girls began to pray and to share and to be support for themselves and others. They knew they had found a focus.

But, how do we know to whom we should listen? What happens if we allow someone into our inner circle? We let them know who we are and where our vulnerable points may be. It is the most amazing experience when the right person is there, but it can be most disheartening if the wrong person becomes our confidante.

We sometimes find someone we trusted has betrayed our secrets. We thought we knew them. We counted them among the select few who understood us and cared about us. Can you imagine Jesus and His Disciples as Judas softly kissed the Master's cheek? Or, Brutus as he faced Caesar? What betrayals those were!

Have you ever faced betrayals in your own life?

Who was it?

How did you discover they did not have your well-being on their agenda?

How did you react to the revelation?

Remember the egg and the carrot? Which were you when crisis struck? For after all, are there many situations worse than realizing a friend is not really a friend? And, sadly, the discovery usually comes when we need this person the most. We turn to them, and they have actually vanished.

What has been your reaction to relationships that were disappointing or disloyal?

Were you blessed enough to look in a different direction and see comfort in the eyes of someone else close by?

Or, did you face the situation totally alone?

I have been there. In my eight years of raising my daughters as a single mom, I often found that I so desperately needed attention and a friend that I was not judging wisely what some relationships were really founded upon. More often than I would like to admit, I was looking into the eyes of one who really did not care. They did not want to be bothered when I needed them, and they had little or no understanding of the realities I was facing. I was usually looking into the eyes of what I thought was a would-be husband…a rescuer who, like the proverbial "Knight in Shining Armor," could not wait to come rescue me. WRONG! I had incorrectly looked for understanding and support where none was available. And, in business, I sometimes found people around me who did not understand or care, much less support me. It is a solitary and scarey place to be…out on the limb, alone.

"We outgrow people, places, and things as we unfold. We may be saddened when old friends say their peace and leave our lives… but let them go. They were at a different stage…and looking in a different direction".

Kristin Zambucka
Poet

I urge you to always be realistic about your friendships and your expectations. Never hesitate to meet new people and cultivate existing relationships, but at the same time, listen to that inner voice meant to protect you. Proverbs 28:23 says, "In the end, people appreciate frankness more than flattery."

Close your eyes.

Who do you picture when you see the words friend, supporter, comforter, caregiver?

Are they the same person? Are they long-time or new friends?

What is the foundation of your friendship...work, family, children, charities, religion, politics?

How have you cultivated the relationship?

Do you share everything?

Write your thoughts down and set them aside. Observe your contacts over the next few days and then, look back at what you have written. You will value your relationships and see them more clearly.

We Baby Boomers were given some guidelines in our youth…

"You are judged by the company you keep!"

"Never date someone you couldn't feel comfortable marrying!"

"The way you dress tells what kind of person you are!"

We thought these sayings were simplistic, but in the years of unique friendships and challenging relationships, I have come to see the truth in these old adages. Ask yourself if you believe these three to be true.

> *"Humility is the acceptance of the possibility that someone can teach you something else you do not know about yourself. Conversely, pride and arrogance, close the door of the mind."*
> *Arthur Deikman*
> *Physician Studying Meditation*

When a tragic fire struck a Rhode Island nightclub overflowing with enthusiastic young adults, many people died because they were trapped in the overwhelming smoke and flames. One man, Harold Pensiero, escaped the fire in the early moments of the turmoil. Yet, as he stood outside helpless to save anyone, he could here the screams of someone looking for a way out. The smoke was so blinding that those trying to escape could not find a doorway. At that instant, Harold knew that he had to do something. He reached for the snow at his feet and began making snowballs. He hurled into the inferno toward the screaming voice. "Just follow the snowballs," he shouted, and he kept hurling the white clumps of wetness into a seemingly hopeless death trap. Suddenly, a man emerged from the smoke drawn by the improbable path of snowballs. The two men did not know each other. Would that we all be surrounded by friends like Harold Pensiero!

Two women were walking down the streets of New York City. It was a glorious evening, and they had just finished dinner at the Russian Tea Room. They grabbed a cab and headed back to the apartment where they were staying. It was tiny but right in the heart of Manhattan. As they turned the corner on 41st Street, they nearly tripped over a large pasteboard box. Deep in conversation, they almost didn't notice the foot protruding from the corner of the box. They stopped and looked down at it wondering if someone had died and fallen there. Then, they heard it. The snoring or was it gasping for air? They weren't sure. As they stood there wondering what to do, the box moved. More of the man's body was visible, and he was obviously poorly dressed. They looked around to see if anyone else noticed this homeless person lying in the heart of New York City. People were passing by, but no one seemed to understand or care. He was just another piece of garbage waiting to be thrown onto the City's dump. The women looked at each other again and decided there was nothing they could do. They rationalized that he was obviously passed out or asleep or maybe even comatose. They were from a small town in Kentucky, and they were leaving the next day. No one would expect them to do anything. No one would notice if they didn't do anything, so they turned and headed up the stairs to their apartment.

"He who has beautiful roses in his garden, must have beautiful roses in his heart."

S. R. Hole
Author

Why wouldn't these women do something? Did they think it was someone else's responsibility? Where was this man's support system? To whom could he turn for help? Was there no one who saw the strengths beneath his weaknesses? Two thousand years ago, an itinerate preacher once said, "If you do it unto the least of these, you do it unto me!"

Surround yourself with people who understand and care about you! How simple that is and yet how dramatic the results without it! Surely this homeless man in New York City would not be alone if someone cared…if someone had been around him who understood his needs. Someone surely wondered where he was and would have helped had they been able to find him.

Maybe I'm an optimist! Maybe I'm just naïve! Whatever it may be, I truly believe that the rising number of homeless in this the world's most affluent country would be greatly diminished if only everyone had someone to care. If only everyone had someone surrounding them with understanding and the willingness to sacrifice themselves for another person's well-being, it would make a huge difference.

You may never have been close to being homeless. You may never have lost a job. You may never have experienced someone in your office stabbing you in the back. How very blessed you are to not know the taste of these things firsthand. It is a devastating place to be in life when you realize there is no one to turn to when you are in need, but it is even more devastating to turn to someone and have them not be there for you. I urge you to evaluate the people in your life. Consider the author, Reshad Field's quote, "Whenever we communicate with each other correctly, there is an exchange of energy." When you look at the people in your life...

Determine what holds your relationships together.

Determine what positive aspects of your personality are enhanced by the time you spend with them.

Consider what you bring to their lives.

What are the keys to their success?

Are you there when they need you?

Do you anticipate your time with them?

What do you expect when you first see them?

Once upon a time in my life, I lost nearly everything that I had. With three daughters and no home, I reluctantly turned to my parents for support. They were not only willing, but also anxious to help. They provided money, a home, and even job opportunities. But, I let my pride and my stubbornness interfere with my common sense. I thought I had to be superwoman and do it all by myself. So, after less than a year, I abandoned all that my parents had given me and moved my children into a small apartment. What would I have done had my mother and father not stepped in to help me? Would I have been abandoned on the streets? Would I have been alone? Would I have been scrounging for food? I know that I would not have. Why? Because all through my life, I have been blessed with people who care...not only my family, but also friends who checked on me and worried about me, who offered jobs, who cared for my daughters.

"Make New Friends, but Keep the Old!" The truth in this Girl Scout song is timeless and ever essential to nourishing our inner self. Never forget that God often places new friends in our path. Our greatest loss is to pass them by unheeded. Our greatest joy is to have them join our journey.

Watch for the strangers who enter your life with words of wisdom. They represent a God who cares and understands. Then, continue to surround yourself with those who understand, care and support you! How amazingly beautiful your life will be with these people beside you!

CHAPTER SEVEN

Without the Valleys of Life, There Are No Mountaintops!

"Your greatest life messages and your most effective ministry will come out of your deepest hurt."

Rick Warren
Author, The Purpose Driven Life

The phone rang as I was working at my desk. It was my secretary saying my mother needed to talk with me. "Hi, Mom!" "She did it, Donnie!" The anguish in her voice was deafening. I couldn't say a word as she continued. "I found her this morning. She's gone!" She was sobbing now, and my father took the phone. I could feel the knot tightening in my throat.

"Your sister is gone. She died today." I was shocked, but why? She had been threatening suicide for nearly a year and had even tried unsuccessfully several times. Why hadn't I listened? Why hadn't I tried to help? Why didn't I take her threats seriously? I just could not believe she had really done it.

Peggy was a wonderfully giving woman who had never been married. She was an accomplished athlete riding her stallion bareback, winning at triathlons and loving to water ski. She was very intelligent... salutatorian of her high school class, magna cum laude from college and in the process of finishing her PhD in economics. So, how could this happen? How could we lose someone so amazing? It was simple. She never accepted the fact that she WAS so amazing and that she was deeply loved! Manic depression is a horrible disease.

That was 1993, and we have survived the loss of my sister, but still miss her presence in our lives. We have looked for understanding and meaning. We have prayed daily for peace. What we have found are chances to share her life with others. Because of Peggy's death, a sixteen-year-old girl was able to admit her own thoughts of suicide. She saw the pain and the worthlessness of this act. This confident, young woman lives and is a nurse today striving to console others in crisis.

Because of the love my parents had for Peggy, a park now exists with softball fields, picnic areas and walking paths. She would have cherished this, and I have no doubt that she smiles down upon it each day.

Sadly, there have been other horrifying days. Five year's later, my brother's daughter, age sixteen, and my husband's 24-year-old niece died suddenly in separate car accidents just ten weeks apart. There will forever be a hole in our family's collective heart, but through the horror of these losses have emerged monumental moments of growth. Commitments to appreciate our loved ones and treasure each time we are together. These are the legacies of our losses. My daughter Billi found writing allowed her to deal with and release the emotions of our valleys...

Accept the Truth That Without Valleys, There are no Mountaintops!

BILLI'S LETTER

With the tragedies that have faced me in my life, I should be many things that I am not. I should be introverted. I should be cold. I should be pessimistic. I should be hateful and faithless. I should be vengeful, and I should feel very alone. But I don't! As I have grown older, I made a very important decision. I decided instead of being afraid and mad at the world for the rest of my life, I am going to live life for all it's worth.

When I was two years old, my parents got divorced which forced me to grow up fast. My character blossomed, and I began to attain a great sense of humor. The realization of growing up without a father was hard, but I gained a positive attitude when my mom married my awesome stepfather.

I reached the end of seventh grade to find out my idol, my Aunt Peg had committed suicide. She was the one I looked up to as a "mother figure" while my mom was a "working dad." My mom's sister was diagnosed with manic-depression six months earlier. Her death left me with a heavy heart, but a line from her favorite song reminded me that I would make it through. The lines, "Sometimes it takes a rainy day to let you know that everything is going to be okay" taken from the Chris Williams song, "Waterfall" became a motto for my life.

I remembered that line when I was faced with my grandfather's death my freshman year in high school. My father was glad to hear such comforting words from the song. I was sad, but I saw the great influence that my grandfather had on my life, and then, I regained my strength. I made it to my sophomore year when a friend of my sister's committed suicide after struggling with depression. My school and family were shocked and struck by the "deja vu."

That summer, I became a Christian and started regaining my trust in God. For a year and a half, everything was going as planned. I was a Senior in high school when I decided to be a junior leader for my youth group. Christmas came around, and I was overjoyed with the Holiday Season. Then, the second week in January, I went on a ski trip to upstate New York. The second night I was there, I called home to hear the news that my maternal grandmother was in the hospital with a blood clot in the back of her brain. It was small enough to be dissolved naturally, but I was worried sick. She ended up going home the next day and is still fine today.

But, when I arrived home on Martin Luther King Day, 1998, my mom said she needed to have a serious talk with me. After realizing that I was not in trouble for having done something wrong, my mom told me the most horrifying news of my life. She explained to me that my only girl cousin on her side of the family had been tragically killed in a car accident at the age of sixteen. My goals in life suddenly changed. I was inspired to climb for the highest peaks and to live on the edge. My departed cousin Rachel always told me that it would be "so great" to go to college in Colorado, even if it was 1500 miles away from home. I am so glad I decided to go there.

I started searching for the positive side in everything that confronted me when even more of life's hardships hit me. Exactly ten weeks after Rachel's death, my stepfather's only niece was killed in a car accident at the age of 24. Another "deja vu." I could not believe that all this could be happening to one family. I fought through the tears and relied heavily on my faith to survive this latest nightmare. I made it out alive and soon after, graduated from high school. Two days afterwards, my favorite teacher died of pancreatic cancer. He was a well-known high school track coach and motivator whose words of wisdom guided every one of his students and athletes. He told me that I would only be successful if I enjoyed my career, no matter what it might be. I took that to heart and will always hold it dear.

My mom has always told me that "God will only give us as much as we can handle", and I believe that! Someone else once said "It doesn't matter how deep or cold the water, you still have to go through it!"

I am still standing strong and positive after all the things I have been tested with.

Beyond this mature wisdom, I have heard my daughter Billi tell people time and again that "Everyone has suffering in their lives, but it is the way we handle the situations which make all of us who we are today."

Have you experienced devastating loss? How did you face it?

Accept the Truth That Without Valleys, There are no Mountaintops!

Where did you gather the strength for climbing out of the depths of despair to live again?

When you face today's world, are you willing to accept the truth that without the valleys of life, there are no mountain tops?

Imagine a life where everything is void of problems, challenges or pain. It would be so wonderful and peaceful. Or would it? Would we grow, would we learn, would we become stronger if we only experienced victories? I contend that I have grown more from the time that I was fired than when I was successfully working at the height of my career.

"When we long for life without difficulties, remind us that oaks grow strong in contrary winds and diamonds are made under pressure."

Peter Marshall
Chaplain, U.S. Senate

A few months after the terrible attacks on the World Trade Center, I went to New York. I couldn't stop thinking about this city that I loved so much and what this tragedy might have done to its collective psyche. My dream was to understand and in some way help. So, with still and video cameras in hand and a notepad always open, I walked the streets talking with total strangers about how their lives...their dreams...had changed forever.

What would America be like today had September 11, 2001 never occurred...

TO A FRIEND
JANUARY 26, 2002

I had to come. You have been my friend for twenty years, and you have been wounded. Why it took me four months to show you I cared, I cannot explain. I had watched as you were struck and struck again. I cried for you and prayed for your recovery. I watched in awe as you rose up defiantly from such unimaginable pain. I wanted to come, but I didn't know how I could help.

You greeted me like everything was just the same as before. You were still beautiful and vibrant and exciting. You were confident, but quieter. You seemed genuinely pleased that I had returned, and you didn't seem to care that I was late in coming. You were just grateful that I cared.

You are the same...and yet, you are not. Your shaken spirit has emerged stronger and wiser. Your scar is now a symbol of your resilience and your deepening faith. You are still my dear, special friend.

I walked your paths, heard your music and witnessed the vibrancy of your being. I photographed your face in all its emotions and angles. I saw your angels as they hovered all around to protect you. I wiped away tears as I felt your pain and your loss. I smiled as I listened to your children's laughter and smelled the fragrance of your fabulous meals. I applauded your theater and your art, your fashion and your glitter.

And, as I flew away, wanting to stay with you so much longer, the light of your resolve was visible for all the world to see. That special light is your gift to an anxious world, and it shines high into the heavens marking the place where your heart was broken.

New York City, you will always be my friend and a friend to millions. But, now you are so much more. You are the epitome of faith and peace and love...the kind of friend that each of us prays will be in our lives forever!

God bless you, my friend!

Accept the Truth That Without Valleys, There are no Mountaintops!

Congresswoman Deborah Pryce is the fourth ranking member of the United States House of Representatives. One day, Deborah and her husband learned that their daughter had an extremely rare form of cancer. After a year of heroic struggles and unimaginable pain, Caroline slipped away at only nine years of age. Her funeral brought together her young classmates and the government's most powerful leaders. The loss was so devastating that all who celebrated Caroline's life that day, shed tears for a little child gone too soon.

The valley was so unimaginably deep. The determination to find a mountaintop was undaunted. And, now, **HOPE STREET KIDS** exists, created as a tribute to Deborah's child. In less than four years, a national foundation in Caroline's memory has raised more than four million dollars for doctors researching childhood cancers.

HOPE STREET KIDS

Just five years ago, we assumed that cancer was an adult's disease. At that time, we didn't conceive that kids even got cancer. Then in 1999, our family's world was turned upside down, and we entered a very real and terrifying world of pediatric cancer. What at first we thought might be simple growing pains in our daughter's leg ended up being our worst nightmare. Our daughter Caroline Pryce Walker was diagnosed with neuroblastoma, a rare, aggressive cancer. After a year-long battle, we lost our precious daughter at age nine.

The tragic death from cancer of our daughter Caroline was the beginning of a crusade for us. The program we founded, **HOPE STREET KIDS***, grew out of lively banter between Caroline, other children undergoing treatment for cancer and their parents in the activity room of Memorial Sloan Kettering Cancer Center in New York City. We all wanted to spare other families the fear, anger and isolation that a diagnosis of cancer brings. We were ignited into action that day, filled with determination and hope. Caroline, who was courageously fighting her cancer, was excited and optimistic about the future. We named the program that afternoon and proclaimed its mission. "Just think how many kids we could save, if we had a million dollars," Caroline said.*

Today, under the auspices of one of the nations' leading cancer research and education organizations, the Cancer Research and Prevention Foundation, **HOPE STREET KIDS** *has been shaped from*

Caroline's idea and our heartfelt desire to continue the fight she began. We have channeled our energies into this endeavor to make a real difference in the lives of other children while keeping Caroline's wonderful spirit alive by creating something positive in her name. We believe we can truly help families of children with cancer, fund cutting-edge research and find effective cures and have an effect on the health and well being of all children in the United States. This is our fervent desire -- and our promise to Caroline.

There are many challenges that lie ahead in the war on pediatric cancer. We are dedicated to continuing the fight Caroline began, and we are dedicated to honoring her memory and to honoring lives of each child affected by cancer.

Four years after Caroline's death, Deborah would reflectively say, "Everything in life has a different perspective now. Mine has a deeper spirituality than ever before."

Families who have lost children deal with an unnatural order of nature. Parents should leave this earth long before their children. Congresswoman Pryce represents the millions of families throughout the world who have dealt with such a loss. She, like so many of them, is an inspirational example of how we must move on and find purpose in what has happened.

Without the valleys of life, there would be no majestic mountaintops!

The valleys can be less devastating than the loss of a child or sister, but they are valleys nonetheless...

Jeff Smoker, the extremely talented 2003 Michigan State quarterback, is just one of millions of people who face personal challenges...deserts of despair. Jeff admitted alcoholism while still in college and began the grueling climb to sobriety. He is now near the summit of his mountaintop as he continues to quarterback one of the best football programs in the United States.

I know a single mother who lost her job. She had applied for unemployment six weeks after because she was too proud to go immediately. She was interviewing frantically, because she was not getting her child support, and her Masters in teaching was worthless since no positions were open. Through her parents and friends, she heard about a job in a large hospital. She was asked to interview, but after waiting for two hours, the meeting was postponed. It was an agonizing week before she heard about the new appointment, and, again, she waited nearly two hours only to have a brief twenty minutes with the head of the hospital, Pat Davis. Pat seemed impressed, but she gave this young woman an assignment and asked her to return in three days.

The Mom worked hard on the sample of her work knowing a new job rested on the results of her efforts. But, she also made an appointment for Aid to Dependent Children just because she had no money. When the time came for the second interview, she was ready and confident. She walked in, portfolio and project in hand. Pat greeted her politely and studied the woman's work eagerly. After a few comments, Pat came quickly to the point, "We have decided not to open the position I was interviewing you for." The mother's heart sank. She had hit so many brick walls, and she did not want to accept welfare. She fought back the tears as Pat continued. "But, we have decided to broaden the job to include Marketing and PR for the entire hospital, not just the Heart Institute." This Mom had never had such a large responsibility, so she assumed she was being let down easy.

She was wrong..."I would like you to begin as soon as you can and the salary will be..." She didn't even hear the amount. It really didn't matter. The Mom...soon to be spokesperson for an international medical phenomenon...just knew she had a job. She rose quite professionally, shook Pat's hand and as she was thanking her, burst into tears and raced around behind the desk to give Pat a hug.

Two months later, Dr. William DeVries came to that hospital and for the next four years, the medical community and most of the United States was focused on the implantation of a new Artificial Heart there. That was my mountaintop in 1984 after the deep valleys of being fired and surviving a nasty divorce.

Ah, Divorce! It is such a part of our society. The divorce rate in America exceeds 50%. What a valley this is for not only the cou-

> *"Forgiving is not forgetting. It is just letting go of the hurt."*
>
> Mary McLeod Bethune
> Educator

ple, but also family and friends! How we face this particular valley will determine our future. We can be angry at our mate or committed to using our emotions in a positive way that will strengthen our resolve for a new beginning.

And what about the children of divorce? A book entitled ***The Unexpected Legacy of Divorce; A Twenty-five Year Landmark Study*** by Judith Wallerstein contains research about children in divorced families nearly two decades ago. The author initially did a study about the children, but years later ran into one of the young women she had once interviewed. After speaking with her, Wallerstein was compelled to revisit some of the other children she had worked with, now that they were adults. She then identified adults who as children had lived near her study group but whose parents had not separated. These people had even been in the same grade. She looked at the adult lives of both groups, focusing on decisions about jobs, marriage and independence while assessing their current lifestyles.

The results were telling. Clearly, the children of divorce had an improbable resilience. They appeared slower in making choices about colleges, careers and mates. In their formative years, the study suggests these kids were busy facing the emotional valleys of their parents' decisions. The children of divorce seemed to question their own self-worth and the choices they were facing. Some had to learn how to verbalize what often traumatized them. Yet, the study revealed that, in general, children of divorce were making better choices, because they were taking longer and being more deliberate about where their lives were going. Could it be that the valley of the Baby Boomer divorce surge will reveal a towering mountain of stronger, more devoted marriages?

I urge you to look across any of those valleys in your life…death of someone you loved dearly or loss of a job…failures in your emotional life or demise of a friendship…and learn from that deep place.

Why did it happen?

Accept the Truth That Without Valleys, There are no Mountaintops!

What was your role in it?

Can you find some positive outcome in your future?

Will you let those who love you help?

Do you allow yourself to pray?

You are special! In the midst of the valley, it is impossible to believe that, but you are! Find the inner strength to survive, to climb higher and higher atop the rim of that spectacular mountain. Sing, smile, gaze at a sunset, touch the hand of someone you love, but, most importantly, let yourself cry! Tears are our cleansing. They release the emotions that are so deeply buried within. They provide the letting go we need to turn our face from looking downward to looking to the heights of our future.

What valley have you walked out of?

What mountaintop have you reached, because you turned toward the heavens?

Remember that the dark path can suddenly brighten, and the problems will become stepping stones of opportunity, if you believe you are not facing them alone. God has an outstretched hand that will help you climb to a glorious summit. And, from there, you will look down and see only beauty.

CHAPTER EIGHT

Believe There is a Hole in Your Heart
That Only God Can Fill!

"Everything else can wait, but not the search for God!"

George Harrison
The Beatles

COINCIDENCE

She was sick. Nausea had swept over her like a sudden slap, and she could not get past it. She looked out the window at the Colorado landscape. They were east of Denver in the Plains that revealed little color and even less wildlife. She tried to focus on the horizon thinking maybe she was car sick, but she remembered that there had been pains for weeks before she left. Then, she felt the baseball bat hit her in the chest. She could not breathe. She knew what was happening. She didn't want to tell her husband driving the car beside her. He would have to divert his hunting trip that had been planned for a year if she got sick, so she just stayed silent...for nearly an hour.

She could see they were nearing the city. The skyline loomed above, and he began the slow arc onto the new road that would take them around the city out of Denver. The nausea was worse and the pain in her chest...like a truck parked on her stomach...was worsening. She was a nurse. She knew what was happening. Her father had died at the age of 47 of a sudden heart attack. She was 62.

She motioned for her husband to put the window down. She was so short of breath, she could not ask him to do it.

"What?" Her husband of nearly forty-one years was astonished. He thought she was asleep. "Why?'

She simply leaned her head out and lost everything she had eaten in the last 24 hours. But, the pain only increased. She was really scared now and sweating profusely. He knew that stopping the car would lose precious time, so he rushed the car toward the hospital. He had seen a sign just before she got sick.

He couldn't believe it! He was a doctor, but he knew so little about the heart. He was trained as an obstetrician and a gynecologist. One of his dear friends back in Louisville was an outstanding cardiologist, but they were out here in the middle of nowhere with no medical help. This was the era before cell phones, so they had no way to call for help. He rushed toward the exit, as her color became worse and worse, and she closed her eyes. Was she asleep or fading into unconsciousness? He had no idea but did not dare stop until he reached the hospital.

There was the exit, but there was no hospital! He searched desperately for another sign. There it was, barely visible across from the

Believe There is a Hole in Your Heart That Only God Can Fill!

exit with an arrow sending him south. That's away from the city, he thought. What kind of place will this be?

Then, he saw it. A non-descript Army hospital...Fitzsimmons Army Base Hospital...just ahead. He urged the car faster looking again at this woman he had met at Johns Hopkins Medical School decades ago and loved ever since.

He pulled the car straight up to the door marked EMERGENCY and tried to whisper calmly, "I will be right back with a doctor." And, he was. The nurses and the doctor rushed out with a gurney and helped her onto the bed. She was in such pain now that she was having trouble breathing.

The examination went fairly quickly because all the signs were right. She was in the early stages of a heart attack, but they had given her medication to ease the pain. There were at least six nurses and medical corpsmen as well as two doctors attending her.

The cardiologist looked at Hal. "She needs to be catheterized now to see what has happened. She will probably need surgery right away, but first we have to see what is going on with her heart."

Hal thought, "No way am I going to let a total stranger, especially at some military base, perform procedures on my wife." He was too scared to remember that once upon a time, he too had been a physician at a military hospital in Tucson, and he was a "damn good one" as his commanding officer once told him.

Outloud, he said, "Dr. Miller, I can't believe it is so urgent. We can stabilize her and get her on a plane back to Louisville where my friend who is a cardiologist, can evaluate her."

"Sir, you don't understand."

"I guess I don't," he thought, but time was wasting. "I need to use your phone to call our doctor." He would call Hank Post and see what he thought was the best thing to do.

It seemed like an hour before the receptionist got Dr. Post on the phone. In reality, it was less than two minutes. "Hank, it's Hal Baker. Julie is in the emergency room just outside of Denver, and the doctor says she is having a heart attack. He wants to do a catheterization and thinks she urgently needs surgery. I don't know these people. Would you talk to the doctor and help me decide how to handle this? Julie is really sick!"

Hal handed the phone to the doctor and walked back to the room where they had put her. She was resting quietly, but he was so afraid. Their lives together had been filled with ups and downs, but they had always seemed to come through stronger. He had a sinking feeling that things may be different this time. The doctor knocked on the door. "Hank wants to talk to you."

Had he not been so focused on Julie, Hal might have noticed the doctor using his friend's first name instead of his title, Doctor. The panic in Hal's face was overridden only by his fear that there may not be a doctor for many, many miles, much less a decent one.

"Hal, let Dr. Miller do whatever he thinks is best for Julie." Hal caught his breath and out loud, began to protest, "But, we don't even know this guy!"

Hank interrupted, "It is the most unbelievable coincidence. Dr. Miller was in Louisville for the last four days interviewing for a partnership in our practice here. We had sought him out, because he is excellent, and he will take fabulous care of Julie. Don't worry about anything!" Hal hung up the phone and looked toward heaven. His prayer was filled with gratitude and utter amazement.

Julie would have her catheterization at once.

When finished, Dr. Miller looked at Julie and said, "You are a very lucky young lady. You have more than a 90% blockage in four of your vessels leading to your heart. We are going to have to operate on you immediately."

Julie begged, "Can't I go home and get the surgery done in Louisville where we are good friends with nationally renowned heart surgeons?"

"No, you cannot!" stated Dr. Miller emphatically, "I recommend a doctor who just did my mother's surgery." Weakly, she agreed.

He called and arranged for her procedure to be performed almost immediately. Then, he transferred her to the hospital in Denver.

She would have her surgery. She would recover under the watchful eye of her husband and her three children who had rushed from Louisville to her bedside. She would recover and then fly home a healthy woman living proof that there is a God!

Believe There is a Hole in Your Heart That Only God Can Fill!

A doctor in the middle of Colorado responding to an emergency was the same man who had been recruited by the woman's very own doctor back in her hometown...Irony? Coincidence? Or, the hand of God?

Coincidence is when God chooses to remain anonymous!

> *"Troubles are often the tools by which God fashions us for better things."*
>
> H. W. Beecher
> *Orator, Preacher, Writer*

I believe the most important concept defining our lives is how we feel about God.

As I mentioned in Chapter Six, there is a very tiny book that was on the *New York Times*, non-fiction bestseller list for many months, *The Prayer of Jabez* by Bruce Wilkinson. The theme is quite radical...

GOD WILL GIVE US WHATEVER WE ASK FOR AS LONG AS IT WILL MAKE US BETTER PEOPLE

Sound crazy or sacrilegious? Not so! The book of Chronicles, one of the most monotonous books in the Bible shares a most life-challenging five lines. Jabez prayed...

> *"Oh, that you would bless me indeed and enlarge my territory. That your hand would be with me, and that you would keep me from evil. And God granted his wishes."*

This is the most amazing little prayer...for those of you who already pray, try this one. For those of you who don't pray, just think about it. How radical it would be if it really is acceptable to ask to be blessed a lot...that's "in deed"...and to grow your influence and business...that's "territory"...but also ask God not to leave as you do not want to get cocky or in trouble or ignore those around you who need you. I began praying this prayer three years ago. I repeat it everyday, often more than once.

In the book *The Prayer of Jabez*, there is a scene where a Mr. Jones is greeted at heaven's gate by St. Peter and shown all the glories there. Jones spies a large white building in the midst of the fabulous golf course and lakes and horses and homes and moun-

> *"God's gifts put man's best dreams to shame."*
>
> Elizabeth Barrett Browning
> Author

tains…all the beauty I imagine in heaven. He wants to know what is in the building, but the angel changes the subject. Being human like us all, he can't be satisfied with everything in heaven if he doesn't get to see in this building. So, he persists and finally, the angel allows him to enter. "But you really won't like what you find in there." "Not like something in heaven," Mr. Jones thinks to himself. How could that be? As he enters, he notices a very sterile series of rows with white boxes and big red bows. All the same except for the name on each. The rows are alphabetized, and Mr. Jones races to the J's to grab his box. The angel tries to stop him, but to no avail. As Jones opens it, the Angel softly says, "What you see in there are all the gifts God had waiting for you if only you had asked God for them or recognized they were for you!"

After reading this, I did what the author suggested. I made a list of all that I wanted for my family, my friends and me that would broaden our lives and expand our territories. I asked for three small pages of things, some tangible, some spiritual. All but one on the list has been granted. Amazing!

Wilkinson so patiently tells us in *The Prayer of Jabez*, "We must tell God what we want. Then, be ever vigilant for his response."

What are your gifts?

What should you ask for?

What awaits you in your own special box?

Are you hesitant to ask for what you want for fear God will be angry?

Would parents be angry with a child for asking for a special gift, especially one that makes them so much brighter and valuable to this world? Why would God be any different?

Have you seen the recently posted billboards with the message, "God Speaks?"

As you read these, note your reaction. You will see the relationship you have with God personified in your feelings about these statements…

Tell the kids I love them. God

Keep using my name in vain. I'll make rush hour longer. God

That "Love Thy Neighbor Thing," I meant it! God

Loved the wedding. Invite me to the marriage. God

Let's meet at my house Sunday before the game. God

What part of "Though Shalt Not…" didn't you understand? God

We need to talk. God

My way IS the highway!   God

Have you read my #1 best seller? There WILL be a test. God

Do you have any idea where you are going? God

Don't MAKE me come down there! God

> *"My imperfections and failures are as much a blessing from God as my successes and my talents, and I lay them both at His feet."*
>
> *Mahatma Gandhi*
> *Hindu Leader*

How did you feel as you read these? Did you smile? Did you conjure up the image of God sitting on His heavenly cell phone talking to you? What notepad might He be jotting these jolting thoughts down on?

As we face life's challenges, it never hurts to remember that God promises a safe landing, not a smooth ride.

With the world constantly throwing us some pretty unique and often unexpected curve balls, I find it helpful to look for the reason and the message in the situation. Maybe it is true that coincidence is when God chooses to remain anonymous. Would that give you some solace on those days when you are scratching your head about why things happen as they do? It helps me find some meaning and look for the lesson.

Often, I find myself inspired by a comment or a sentence in an article or a spectacular sunrise. God renews us so many ways, but we must be ever alert to these unexpected reassurances.

In 1999, Mayor Rudy Giuliani was on top of the world. He was set to run for the Senate and for all you Republicans, the experts thought he would win. Then, he found out he had cancer, and a few days later, his extramarital relationship was made public. For weeks, he kept on the positive line that he could run. He would run! But, his health and the non-stop news coverage caused him to end his candidacy. When he did in May, 2000, he said...

"New York is my deep passion. Sometimes things happen in life for reasons you don't know until afterwards."

How prophetic...what would New York City be if Rudy had not led the City as it faced those horrific challenges of 9/11? His steely determination was the underpinning of his city's return to its strength and power.

"I believe in God." Rudy said during a Barbara Walters' interview a few months after the terrorists attacked the World Trade Center. "Somehow, someway, all of this was part of a divine plan." Whether you agree with him or not, his faith has been his strength through all this tragedy.

Believe There is a Hole in Your Heart That Only God Can Fill!

And, then there is the irony of my sister who died in 1990 and the horror of September 11. On that crisp blue morning, I was quietly remembering that it would have been her 48th birthday.

From these tragedies, I have adopted the thought that I will not put a question mark where God puts a period.

Many times, it is in prayer that I find my greatest reassurance and renewed energy. It is like making a phone call to a cherished friend to share my deepest thoughts and concerns. As writer Catherine Marshall says, "The purpose of all prayer is to find God's will and to make that will our prayer." God's will, our prayer! Isn't that a comforting to know there is a higher power controlling our lives? I have often said how sad it would be if my decisions were the final answer to all my questions.

ANGELS AMONG US!

The country music group, Alabama, has a great song that says, "I believe there are angels among us, sent down to us from somewhere up above. They come to you and me in our darkest hour, to teach us how to live, teach us how to give, to guide us with the light of love."

Now, the idea of angels is so popular right now that it could almost be described as a fad. Some people expect their angels to come in the traditional sense. There was a man living by the Mississippi River during the floods of the mid-nineties. A rescue team rowed up to the front porch of his house and said, "You need to climb in so we can take you to dry land." "Thanks," he said. "But, God is going to rescue me."

They rowed off shaking their heads. They knew, as well as the man did, that the water was still rising. Now, it was above the front porch and about a foot high on his first floor. The Coast Guard rushed up in their motor boat. "Climb in, sir. There is a mandatory evacuation."

"Can't make me go. God is going to save me." And, he proceeded to head to the second floor.

"I believe that friends are quiet angels who lift us to our feet when our wings have trouble remembering how to fly."
Kimberly Dresch
Artist, NBC News Technician

By now the water was above the second story windows, and he had climbed up to the pinnacle of the roof. Trying not to sound doubtful, the man prayed aloud as he looked heavenward. "God, I trust you. When will you send your angels to lift me up to safety?"

Just then, a helicopter hovered over him. They dropped a rope and shouted for him to grab hold. For a third time, he rejected the rescuers as he waited for the Angels of God. An hour later, the house was totally submerged and the man drowned.

When he walked through the pearly gates, he humbly approached God and asked, "Sir, I believed in you. Why didn't you rescue me?" God patiently smiled and said, "Remember the row boat and the coast guard officers and how about the helicopter? Which of my angels did you not recognize?"

How often have God's angels been right in front of you...and you never even knew it?

> "God meets me where
> I am...if I am just
> willing, He will
> come to me".
> *As We Understood*
> *Alcoholics Anonymous*

I know a woman who has an angel party every Christmas to remind her friends of what they have meant to her. Whether you are a religious person or not, you do have a hard time explaining some things any other way than there are angels wandering around ready to help. Let's look again at September 11, 2001.

There were so many stories impossible to explain. Consider the five firemen helping the woman down the stairs. She couldn't go any further, and they were just to three or four floors from the bottom when the tower came crashing down. All of them were found alive with everything above and below totally destroyed.

Believe There is a Hole in Your Heart That Only God Can Fill!

ANGELS???

What about the principal of a high school who calmly ushered her hundreds of students as far away from the buildings as she could into a nearby park. She didn't know that her sister was at that moment perishing in the collapse. She looked across the sea of frightened young people and from out of nowhere, there were strangers passing water and surgical masks to ALL the kids. No one ever saw those people again.

ANGELS???

You know hundreds of other stories about that day and the days that followed, and I know they made you pause…maybe even weep. We want to believe that like that old draft horse, Buddy, we've got others around helping us pull our load.

Take a moment and think about your life…the things you have accomplished, the things you have endured. Where were those "angels among us?"

ANGELS AMONG US!!!!!

Have you ever NEARLY had an accident? One second here, one second there and oh, how different life might have been.

She had been driving for only six months. Her little red car was one week old. She was going the speed limit on the six-lane highway. She was concentrating hard on staying the speed limit while keeping pace with the other traffic. Suddenly, she heard the thundering crash and felt the steering wheel lurch to the left. In a split second, she was propelled into the lane next to her where cars a second before had been racing past at nearly 70 miles an hour. If she had had time to think, she would have known that she was near death when miraculously, the car to her left swerved away from her and into the huge median protecting the west bound from the eastbound lane. The woman behind the wheel was desperately struggling to avoid hitting the girl's little red car while averting a head on collision on the other side of the grassy area she was roaring through. Amazingly, all the cars came to rest with everyone involved safe. Badly shaken, the teenager emerged from the wreckage and looked at the chaos caused by the man to her right. She was too upset to say anything. She only looked at the woman who had risked her own life by swerving left and realized that even angels drive cars. She never got the woman's name. She never could share the realization of God's hand on all of those involved. No doubt, the woman knew that there would forever be a bond between these two. There was a reason why these people were where they were at the moment they were.

Ask yourself…

Have you been in a situation that should have left you badly injured or maybe even dead yet you walked away unscathed? Were you changed? Could you explain how such a thing might have happened?

How do you feel about the oft-used response to crises, "Things happen for a reason?" Think about this. Your relationship with God may be defined by how you respond.

Remember the Charles Schultz quiz we took earlier? One more question...can you name three situations where the angels were with you?

Do you find that you have inadvertently been someone's angel?

Do you think that God has something for you to do that you fail to realize or understand?

> *God does not guide history and the destiny of man by continually opposing men in the projects they have taken in hand. On the contrary, He lets them act. To all appearances, they are acting simply according to their plans, and yet, they cannot avoid becoming the instruments of God and acting in reality according to His plan."*
>
> *Gerhard Van Rad*
> *German Biblical Scholar*

HE WOKE ME EARLY...

God woke me early this morning and said, "Let's go for a walk."

I could hear the waves, so I opened my eyes expecting to see the glistening beach. All I saw was a dark gray fog covering everything. I closed my eyes to get a bit more sleep, because, after all, it was only seven a.m. and I was on vacation.

Yet, in the still of the early morning, a small voice persisted. "Come on. What else do you have to do today? Let me show you what's out there." So, I dutifully rose, put my swimsuit on with shorts and shirt over it and headed down the elevator to the beach. My "walk" began the minute my shoes touched the sand.

I headed straight for the water. The fog was so heavy that I really couldn't see the Gulf until I was about twenty yards from the edge. The sound and smell of the water was more refreshing than I remembered from yesterday's sun time. I could see that the fog was clearing only enough to reveal heavy dark clouds and no sun. But, "Let's go!" kept repeating in my head.

Then, I saw them...dolphins just off shore. They were leaping and racing through the water, four of them playing some sort of tag with each other. All along the beach, there were people stopping and pointing. What beautiful, peaceful creatures they are!

Believe There is a Hole in Your Heart That Only God Can Fill!

On I went, looking down at the sand always wondering what the sea would lay in my path. And, again I saw a wonder of God. Perfect starfish, not one or two, but five, lying on the dry land, destined to die when the sun finally broke through the grayness.

I carefully picked the first one up and walked it into the surf. Then, I took a few more steps, picked up the next starfish, repeating my rescue mission. I continued doing this until I could see they were all safely back home again. Was my walking partner smiling?

A lady, watching my efforts, stopped to ask if I planned to save all the starfish on the beach. I smiled, but before I could answer, she continued speaking. "I just walked down by the end"...she meant Cape Marco about a mile south of where we stood..."There were three carnations that had just washed onto the shore. I nearly cried," she said, "thinking that they were probably washed up from yesterday's boating accident." She paused, and to my surprise, I felt a knot forming in my throat. "I kept walking, and then I doubled back," she continued. "Someone had put the carnations together in the sand and drawn a heart around them..." Her voice cracked. Her eyes filled with tears and so did mine. People had drowned yesterday right off shore while all of us basked in the sun. She ambled on down the beach.

I was just taking a walk because God woke me up and asked me to. I walked on, spying the hundreds of beached conchs, struggling to dig their way back to the water. Yes, I picked them up, at least as many as I could and pitched them back into the waves with the fish. There were so many. I had to accept the fact that I couldn't save them all. I just had to give it a try.

The north end of the island was about a half mile away. I had already walked over an hour and anyway, I wasn't in charge of this stroll. I was just following the Leader.

A five-pronged starfish, absolutely perfect and very tiny lay in the tide pool just to my left. It was not like the earlier large ones with six and eight legs. This one was truly a star. I wanted to take it, but I knew I should not. It would live and thrive there as along as no one else coveted its beauty and took it home. Just beside it was an industrious twosome...hermit crabs fighting over an empty conch shell they both had planned to inhabit. I could have watched them for a long time, but He was urging me to walk on.

I started wondering if this might be the day I would find a sand dollar for Mom. A year before, she had asked me to search the beach for her favorite sea souvenir, but I had never been lucky. Was this why God awakened me early to walk with Him?

Half a mile more and I was nearing the point where the river met the Gulf. Boats of all shapes and sizes headed out for the peacefulness of the sea. As I gazed at all the beauty, I looked down just to avoid the tide, and there before me were two nearly perfect sand dollars. How amazing! I almost missed them. They had the embedded five-sided flower pedal design and then the four oblong holes. Funny, I never thought of how the sand dollar reflected my family... the five of us...my parents, my brother, my sister and me. But, my sister had died eight years before...now we are four.

I carefully placed the sand dollars in the palm of my open, upraised hand and simultaneously, realized that this is the position people put their hands when asked to open themselves up for God's blessings. I was opening myself to God's blessings. How could I possibly ask or accept any more. He had already been so gracious to me.

I had reached the end of the island. Time to go back. I had been gone almost three hours, and the sun had burned away all the fog and clouds. It was hot, and I realized that I had probably sweated off all my sun block. Would it really matter? I peeled off my shirt.

I started walking really fast, taking no time to throw the stranded conchs back to the sea and only pausing momentarily to view my fighting hermit crabs. To my dismay, the tiny starfish was gone. Some other walker had made it a treasure. Why was I in a hurry? "We are having such a good time, God. Why am I so anxious?" My back was hurting, and I could feel my chest roasting. I put my thin shirt back on and tried walking backwards.

I was about half way home at the Residence Beach, when I turned around and began walking forward. I searched the waters for more dolphins or even a graceful stingray, but I saw nothing. The little children laughed as they chased the seagulls or tiptoed

Believe There is a Hole in Your Heart That Only God Can Fill!

into the cool of the water. "I really don't know why we are rushing, God. Is my walk really ending?"

No sooner had the words left my mind than I noticed several people huddled to my left. Was that a body they were leaning over? I carefully cradled my sand dollars, one in each hand, as I walked nearer the scene.

There was blood all over the man's face. He had gray hair, a muscular body and steely blue eyes. He was alert, but obviously frightened. He had to be about 75 years old. A lady in a two-piece bathing suit was leaning over him trying to stop the bleeding and cool his head with a wet paper towel. I started to walk on, but that still small voice stopped me. Was there something I could do? Was there something I was supposed to do?

The towel was now soaked in blood, and the lady was looking around. I carefully shifted my precious sand dollars and slipped my shirt off of my bathing suit. "Can you use this?" She thanked me, and so did he. But, his eyes never left my face. I walked around the people who were holding a towel up to block the sun from the old man's face and knelt down next to him. "Are you staying here on the island?" I asked. Earlier in the day, I had wondered what would happen if I got sick or hurt while I walked the beach...I had no ID. Would anyone ever find out who I was?

He kept staring at me, then, said, "No. I stay at big hotel near airport. My car is at Marriott."

"You are obviously from Europe," I said, trying to keep him focused on something other than the blood streaming down his face and onto the sand at his side. From his accent, I was sure he was German, but I had learned that guessing could prove me wrong and at the same time, insult the foreign tourists.

"I am from Akron."

"I am from Ohio, too. Columbus." He smiled through the pain of his crushed nose. I asked if anyone was with him. He told me he was alone. "My wife is no longer on earth, but I have daughter in California and one...a doctor...in Akron."

The EMS had arrived, and they were all business. What day was it? What medication was he on? Does he remember what happened? Ask him his name, I kept thinking. Find out where he is staying. Show some sensitivity to the fact that he is all alone.

I kept trying to tell the paramedics what little I knew and so did the lady who had first helped him. They weren't focused on that, just on his immediate condition. The helicopter would be landing in two minutes. Everyone would have to clear off the beach. Did that mean us? Weren't we the only friends this old German had in his time of need? I never moved and neither did the people holding the towel or the lady who had known to turn his head to the side as soon as he fell to keep the blood from choking him. Her young daughter kept vigilant watch nearby.

They had put him on a backboard, and just as they put the oxygen mask over his face, he stared at me and said, "My daughter's number 303..." They tightened the mask on his face as he spoke. "He is telling us his daughter's number," I pleaded angrily. "We'll get it at the hospital," they said. I smiled at him and told him I wouldn't be able to remember my own number at a time like this. I thought I saw his eyes soften for just one moment.

Then, the roar of the helicopter and the vicious swirl of the sand interrupted our thoughts. I grabbed his hand as they lifted him off the sand and then, I told him my name was Donna. "I'm Carrie," the other lady said, and this is my daughter..." I didn't hear her name and neither did he for the whir of the blades was so loud.

They rushed him into the belly of the bird and away he went. We all looked at each other and the bloody beach at our feet. I felt the sand dollars still safely in my one palm. I turned to look one more time as the helicopter rushed northward toward Naples, and I felt one of the dollars slide onto the hardness of the beach. The pieces scattered among the multitudes of broken shells.

And, then I saw them...two dolphins no more than forty yards off shore. They leapt into the sky as if to try to touch the giant bird, and then they went under never to surface again. Where had they come from? Where had they gone? We all looked at each other and knew that Mr. Lohmeyer was not alone on his journey.

But, my walk was not yet over. I rushed back to my condo, changed clothes and headed to the hospital to be sure my new friend would not be alone. Funny, I never doubted this was what I was supposed to do. I never got frustrated as I waited with him for six hours as he lay on a gurney in the hallway of the hospital emer-

Believe There is a Hole in Your Heart That Only God Can Fill!

gency room. He would stay for two days to see why he passed out and crashed nose first onto the shell-covered beach. I would retrieve his glasses from the Marco police and if need be, make sure his car was returned to the drop off in Naples. I knew the ER people weren't sure if I was a "con artist" or a kind person, but really, I didn't care. I knew his daughter probably suspected I was up to no good when the doctors informed her some woman was with him...that he was holding a picture that I had given him of me being kissed by a dolphin.

As I prepared to leave him in the hospital's diligent care, in came Carrie and her daughter holding a giant balloon in the shape of a dolphin. We told him the story of the dolphin's unexpected appearance as he flew away and then, Carrie said, "This is my daughter. You didn't meet her, Mr. Lohmeyer. Her name is Erica." I saw his eyes widen, then fill with tears. In broken English, he said, "My wife's name was Erica." We just looked at each other, awed by everything that day.

God woke me this morning and said, "Let's go for a walk!"

Who gave you a wake-up call this morning?

Think of what your first thoughts were when you awoke. Was there someone whispering in your ear...an idea...a solution to a problem...a moment of gratitude for another new day?

Can you really take credit for an awakening thought? I consider that God speaking to me. What would you call these moments?

Tear out the following page, and place it somewhere you will see it every morning. You will smile and be stronger for what lies in your day ahead.

Believe There is a Hole in Your Heart That Only God Can Fill!

GOOD MORNING!

This is God, and I

will be handling all

of your problems today.

I will not need your help.

So, have a

GREAT DAY!

Find a quiet place and ponder these next few statements and questions. Jot down the first thought that enters your mind after reading them...

The highly successful, current coach Jim Tressel of the Ohio State football Buckeyes is a deeply religious man. He professes with great conviction and humility, "I am only one, but I AM ONE!"

We are born with a hole in our heart that can only be filled by God.

If we are created in God's image and one of our most desperate desires is to be loved, what might God's greatest longing be?

If the game of life ended tonight, would I be a winner?

Recently, I had to laugh out loud at an e-mail I received...the content was one simple sentence from a friend..."As long as there are tests in school, there will be prayer in school!" Prayer...it is no more than a conversation with a loving parent or friend.

> *"We all find the Jesus we want, because we know so little about Him."*
>
> Albert Schweitzer
> Missionary Physician,
> Philosopher

Again, I urge you to explore your spiritual self. You cannot be successful without a GOD in your life. There is no way around it. We are programmed with a hole in our psyche that can be filled only by a higher being. Though He is under assault from the American Civil Liberties Union, the Atheists, the disenfranchised and the cynics of the world, God continues revealing Himself through everyday kindnesses, quiet miracles, comfort and...a baby's smile.

As I mentioned earlier, Mel Gibson, one of America's most beloved actors chose to "walk the walk." He believes that Christ is the Son of God and that His sacrifice for the sins of every human being throughout all centuries is the greatest gift ever given. *The Passion Of Christ* launched in the Spring of 2004, has stirred the human heart in a way that I am sure God intended when He set Mel Gibson on this path of love. Yes, the movie is graphic. Yes, it is heart-wrenching and yes, it makes the message of the Gospel almost overwhelming. When I saw it, I knew the ending; I knew the words almost verbatim. I realized that the faces represented our own trauma had we been witnesses. We were there! Our hearts saw the strength of this thirty-three year old man...the Son of God. What a phrase...The Son of God. Could anyone live up to this? Only the REAL one could!

Mel Gibson has taken an extreme amount of criticism not only from his peers and the anxious Jewish community but also from the media. Reporters and editors keep assessing why he produced the movie. "Why would Mel Gibson risk his entire career on such a venture?" The answer does not seem elusive to me. If you believe in God, it seems obvious. Mel Gibson made *The Passion of Christ*, because he was led to do so. And like an obedient, trusting child who has done as his father requested, Mel Gibson's rewards are mind-boggling both financially and most importantly, spiritually. His vision has prompted one of the most impressive public discussions of Christ's impact on the world since Christ's resurrection 2000 years ago. I urge you to see this film and evaluate your reaction to all you see.

> *"We all wish good things to happen, but we cannot just pray, then sit down and expect miracles to happen. We must back up our prayers with action."*
>
> *Freedom From Despair*
> *Al-Anon and Alateen*
> *Newcomer's Welcome*

WHERE WAS HE?

What ever happened to Joseph? Where was he when Jesus was being ridiculed, scourged, tried and crucified? Mary was there with Mary Magdalene and the beloved Disciple John. She tearfully shadowed His every horrifying step. She cradled His brutalized body, as He lay dead to this world. Where was Joseph?

Yet, without this kind man, things would never have been the same. There would be no reason to believe Mary's story of an angel coming to her and revealing that she was THE virgin chosen to bear God's son. Joseph heard from an angel, too. Without Joseph, Mary would probably have been stoned for having no husband. Without him, there would have been no reason to go to Bethlehem. Without him, there would be no lineage to David as the Old Testament had prophesied.

Without Joseph, the child would have been slaughtered in the cruelty of Herod's assault on baby boys. Without Joseph, the family would never have slipped away into Egypt and then several years later, returned to Nazareth. Without this man, Jesus would never have gone to the bustling, imposing metropolis of Jerusalem at the age of twelve and been lost to His parents while He was about "My Father's business." Ironically, this was one year before the traditional transition of Jewish boys into manhood in the ceremony of bar mitzvah.

Had Joseph not been the chosen father and a carpenter, what would Jesus have been? He was nearly thirty when he began to preach. Have you ever wondered what went on in the 18 years between his being lost in Jerusalem and his temptation by the devil in the wilderness? Clearly, Jesus was deeply loved, for his ability to love transcended any human comprehension. God's son...but also the son of man!

So where was Joseph? Had he died, for of course, he was much older than Mary was? History tells us she was probably only 14 when she "bore a son." Could Joseph have been twenty-five or thirty? Probably so, because Jewish men tended to wed later than Jewish girls. The life expectancy in those early times was much less. He would have been probably 55 or 60 when Jesus left His home to become the greatest man ever to walk the face of the earth. Was Joseph dead when his beloved son suffered such unimaginable horror only to be compounded by the cruel death on the Roman cross? Did Joseph lovingly touch God's robe as He watched this abomination from heaven above? Did Joseph comfort God as their son "bore the sins of the world?"

And three days later, when the stone was rolled away, where was Joseph then? The Gospels tell us that Jesus appeared to Mary Magdalene first, then His mother and His disciples. For forty days, Jesus walked the earth proving to all who heard Him that He was "The Risen Lord." The holes were clearly visible in the palms of His hands as I envision Him raising them to speak. He allowed no one to touch Him, we are told, because "I am not of this earth." Did he make an exception for His mother? Did He let her touch His face and cradle Him in her grateful arms? Did He find Joseph and thank him for being a part of the "Greatest story ever told?"

Where was Joseph?

Believe There is a Hole in Your Heart That Only God Can Fill!

Is this another of the millions of lessons that Jesus gives us about life? Is it His way of telling us that no matter where our parents are, no matter how involved with us they are, we have our own mission in life? The absence of one parent at some point in our transformation may not alter God's plan for us. It may only empower us. We are better for what we learn from those who raise us, but in the end, God will lead us to our place in life. We must only be willing to listen and to learn, to laugh and to cry, to accept that we are, like Jesus, to be "about my Father's business!"

Can you imagine the pride Joseph must have felt as God smothered His son Jesus with loving embraces at the gates of Heaven? If Joseph ever wondered why he was born, the answer was clear on that day.

Do not ever believe that you walk through this life alone. Do not accept what so much of our world forces upon us...that we can find our purpose all by ourselves.

I urge you to see this message from heaven and after you do, get down on your knees and ask God if you are on the path He has set for you. If you believe you make your own way in life with the gifts God has given, then pray for the direction He knows will bring you the life you dream of.

May today there be peace within you. May you believe in a God that knows you are exactly where you are meant to be.

God has given us the gifts of free will and grace to face our challenges and places to find peace like mountains and oceans and forests. God has brought us these things!

Find within yourself the inspiration to talk with God and grasp the greatest life that you and He could ever imagine. Never doubt that there is a way through the valleys and that you have within you what it takes to be the most amazing gift given to those who know and love you.

Go ahead, close this book, hug yourself and move into life with the unfailing belief that you will leave a uniquely valuable mark on the world around you!!!

God bless you on this Amazing Journey!

SUGGESTED READING

*The Holy Bible – Life Application
Study Bible...New American Standard*

Bag of Jewels by Susan Hayward

Boundaries by Dr. Henry Cloud and Dr. John Townsend

Courage is Contagious by John Kasich

Courage to Change by Al-Anon Family Groups

Embraced by the Light by Betty Eadie

God's Little Devotion Book for Women by W. B. Freeman Concepts

Gone With The Wind by Margaret Mitchell

Help Yourself by Dave Pelzer

Homecoming by John Bradshaw

Lessons for Leaders by Homer Rice

Moments Together for Couples by Dennis and Barbara Rainey

Praying God's Word by Beth Moore

Seabiscuit by Laura Hillenbrand

Secrets of the Vine by Bruce Wilkinson

Self Matters by Dr. Phillip McGraw

Spare Parts by Renee Fox and Judith P. Swazey

The Bill Schroeder Story by Martha Barnette

The DaVinci Code by Dan Brown

The Left Behind Series by Tim LaHaye and Jerry B. Jenkins

The Prayer of Jabez by Bruce Wilkinson

The Purpose Driven Life by Rick Warren

*The Unexpected Legacy of Divorce; A Twenty-five Year Landmark
Study by Judith Wallerstein*

Traveling Light by Max Lucado

Tuesdays with Morrie by Mitch Albom

What You Feel, You Can Heal by John Gray

To Obtain Additional Copies Of This Book
Please Send In The Following Form With
A Check or Money Order For
$14.95 Plus $3.95 Shipping And Handling To:

DHG Communications
5620 Olentangy River Road
Columbus, Ohio 43235
614-538-8680

Name ———————————————————————

Address ———————————————————————

City ————————————— State ——— Zip —————————

This Book Is A Gift. Please Send To:

Name ———————————————————————

Address ———————————————————————

City ————————————— State ——— Zip —————————

From ———————————————————————

> To order on-line or to find out about arranging to
> have Ms. Glanzman speak at your next event visit
> "www.dhglanzman.com."

Notes

Notes